LIVING WITH MEMORIES

Living with Memories

by Janette Carter

Carter Family Memorial Music Center   1983

Library of Congress Cataloging-in-Publication Data

Carter, Janette.
  Living with memories.

  1. Carter, Janette. 2. Carter Family (Musical
group) 3. Musicians—United States—Biography.
4. Country music—Biography. I. Title.
ML419.C43A3   1983   784.5'2'00924 [B]   83-14418
ISBN 0-89062-152-7
ISBN 0-9611942-0-0 (pbk.)

Design by Winston Potter
Cover photo by Jack Corn, Corn's Photo Service

Produced by Publishing Center for Cultural Resources, NYC

Manufactured in the United States of America

*Dedicated to my children Don, Rita, and Dale Jett;
to my grandchildren Malissia and Justin;
to Gladys, Joe, Helen, June, and Anita;
and to all my family — the Carters.*

Contents

Preface

A lot has been written about "The Carter Family." Their life and their music have made history. This book dwells a lot more on their personal life and how it feels to be the daughter of a famous family. I loved them because they were my people — not because of their fame. Their wealth was small, but they were pioneers in music. Someone had to start this kind of entertainment, and they were among the first.

I can't pinpoint the exact date of each recording session, the source of each song, the fame they accumulated. I was only four when they recorded their first song — "Bury Me Under the Weeping Willow" — in August 1927 at Bristol, Tennessee.

I am no writer; you may be disappointed in this book. I am the daughter of the famous singing Carter Family, and this is my feeble effort to tell just how proud I am of A. P., Sara, and Maybelle Carter.

Acknowledgements

With thanks to the Rockefeller Foundation, whose financial support made this book possible, and to Howard Klein for his encouragement and interest in me as a writer of songs and now of this book. I can never repay Howard for all he's done for me! Equal thanks go to Patricia Windrow Klein for her belief in me, for her artistic advice, and for being one of my best friends. I am grateful to Rita Janette, my daughter, for her secretarial knowl-edge — she helped me immensely with typing and corrected my mistakes in English and spelling, as did Rita Quillen, who also helped with typing. Special thanks go to my sister Gladys Ettaleen for the loan of family pictures, for her advice and love — for always being there! Finally, my thanks to the Publishing Center, especially Mike Gladstone and Lucy Ferriss, and to all who had a part in *Living with Memories*.

Poor Valley

One of my clearest memories is sitting on the ground, damp from an earlier rain. It would soon be fall of the year — you could feel it in the air. From our house over to Little Valley Farm was quite a walk, so I was resting and looking at one of my favorite scenes. The wind blew gently over the golden field of wheat that would soon be harvested. It made me think of a large wave of water — the whole field seemed in motion. The prettiest gold — I wished I had a silk dress the color of the wheat blowing in the late summer wind.

The valley where I was born and raised is called Poor Valley — why the name, I don't know. It lies in a long lay of land between Clinch Mountain and a large hill called the Nob. You walked across that land, or you went through a gap (one of many) along this country road, to Uncle Ermine and Aunt Ora's.

Daddy's farm lay between Albert Carrol's and Uncle Ermine's. There were three small, wood frame houses, rented to farmers who didn't own land. They worked the crops for their own survival, and a portion went to Daddy for the use of the land.

The summers were hot, the winters were cold — this remains in my mind quite clearly. It was very hard, before school, to feed the chickens, hogs, and cows, draw water from a well, and build fires in the old cook stove and the fireplace, too. Always in winter we'd go to Clinch Mountain and drag out wood to be sawed with the old crosscut saw for winter's use. We picked up the pine knots that were dry. To start a fire real fast, they were better than lamp oil. But meantime the lamp had to be filled and the globes kept shiny and clean — to see by, to study our lessons.

I always loved the train. It went by twice a day, and I'd wait to wave at the engineer until it went around the curve to Neal's Store and the Maces Springs Post Office. Then I'd take an old bucket and pick up the little lumps of coal that had fallen off. They made a good hot fire! Much easier than dragging out wood. I walked a lot, along the railroad tracks.

In my memories, my whole world was home — Grandma's house, the store, the school, Mount Vernon Church, the hills, meadows, valleys, old Clinch, and the train.

I remember the fields of wheat. As I'd sit on the hill or walk by the field, the wind rippling through the wheat before harvest was a beautiful sight to me. At harvest all the neighbors would come to help with the big thrashing machine. We'd all have an extra good dinner. Then, when the day was done, mother would fill up the straw tick with the new, fresh, smelling straw — then the feather tick. If only I were a child again to lie down and sleep so sound — hear the old rooster crow at the break of dawn. It didn't matter if the next day was a schoolday or a workday in summer, I was surrounded by love.

About all that separated the valley from the mountain and Nob was the road. It went from Hilton's to Mendota, and wound in and out across railroad crossings like a long snake. There were, I believe, fifteen railroad crossings in a seven-mile run, with the roads leading into our neighbors' houses. You turned off at Neal's store to go to Grandma's house, right at the foot of the mountain. Her house nestled in a field of rocks; the most rocks in the valley were there—a rock pile, really. I worried about cyclones if one hit the valley right. It would be like going into a narrow tunnel—it would have dry cleaned Poor Valley!

I hated to be taken to the valley and fields. Daddy had a way of placing you there and disappearing on one of his other jobs. There was corn to hoe, weeds—crab grass, ragweeds, a lot of weeds it seemed to me—to cut or pull, seeds to plant, tobacco to tend. Of all crops, I hated tobacco. It takes all year to grow! The worms, the suckers—I would get so sick at my stomach. They were fat and green and clung to the leaves. The tobacco was tended very carefully; it would be sold at the end of the year.

It seemed every row was a mile long. Each child had a hoe. After awhile there was a blister on your hand, then a callus—by the time summer was over, your hands were all rough and had corns.

Time dinner came, a cold biscuit looked good to me, cold soup beans, corn on the cob—anything looked good to eat, just so I could rest! When the sun was sinking in the west you could go home. I'd keep looking for Daddy to pick us up and go home. Then we'd do more work before bed. It seemed my childhood was very short and there was too much work.

There was a creek that flowed by our house—a place all dammed up for the crocks of milk to sit and keep cold for us to drink. There were ducks, and I'd wade and search the banks for duck nests. How I loved to see the babies all soft and yellow, swimming behind their mothers! I had a horror of leeches. They clung to the slick rocks, and once, one got on my foot. My brother Joe said, "It will suck all your blood." It wouldn't turn loose, and finally Daddy removed the horrible ugly thing.

A day was set aside in spring to pluck the geese and ducks for feathers to make ticks and pillows. I would hold them while grandma plucked! I hated this day—I just knew they would freeze or die without those feathers. Afterwards they would hit the creek quacking and slapping water.

In the twilight, I'd run and gather lightning bugs in a jar. Then at night I'd lie in bed and watch all the tiny lights, flickering all over the room. They looked like stars!

There was a large cedar in our front yard, and in the spring I'd watch the birds nest and see the tiny eggs. Soon there would be little birds, chirping for their mother flying in and out of the branches with redworms. I always loved the robins, the bluebirds, the wrens; I'd watch the hummingbirds along the fence, where the hollyhocks bloomed.

I loved spring! To walk amid elder bushes and gather the clusters of blackberries, to hear the cool clear water rushing over the rocks in the mountain streams, to watch the minnows swimming and feel the damp, green moss. Where the violets grew, I'd gather a bundle in my hands to give my mother. She'd put them in a glass of water and set this bouquet on the window sill. There was a hill in back of the store, where Jim Thomas lived. He was an old man, and his grandson, Porter, lived with him amid a hillside of purple lilacs and Japanese bushes with tiny red flowers. He had planted a whole hill of these bushes, and they would perfume the valley. Jim was a kind man; he let me take some lilacs to my teachers Miss Hilton and Mr. Groves, and they were given to friends to place on graves at Mount Vernon Church. How I loved to gather them!

Every spring, as sure as the cressa greens grew in the corn fields, Mother prepared us all for summer. She'd drag out those pink worm pills, large enough to choke a horse! I hated them, and castor oil—Lord, how I hated castor oil! It cured everything: colds, headaches, stomach aches, stumped toes. If you vomited, that old bottle was always near my mother's reach, with a large spoon by its side. I kept a lot of pains to myself—I didn't tell anyone when I got sick, but endured my ailments in silence.

Grandma Carter was Molly Bayes and married Robert Carter. She met him at a square dance at someone's house. She's told it over and over—how "He was the most handsome man I ever saw"; and how she told herself, "That's the man I'll marry"; and

MY APPALACHIAN MOUNTAIN HOME

Honeysuckles are blooming round my cabin door.
It's here I will live, I will die,
Where willows will weep, still waters run deep,
Parents' dear hands, to hold and to guide.
My pathway to manhood, the road will be long.
Appalachian tear drops will fall.
I'll walk, oh so proud, on my land I'm allowed.
I feel I'm the richest of all.

My family, my Jesus, my memories and dreams
Are entwined in a house on the hill.
The mountains, the streams, green pines tall and lean
Surround me so calm and so still.
In my Appalachia, my neighbors are kind.
They love me if I'm right or wrong.
Though others walk tall, I feel very small.
I praise God each day with a song.

A stranger—they pity the farmers, the mines,
His struggles, poverty always there,
A man and his plow, a weathered dear brow,
A family all knitted by prayer.
The fragrance of lilacs on Jim Thomas Hill,
The meadows a carpet of green.
Appalachia, my home—all I'll ever own.
Rare beauty, the land of my dreams.

In writing this for a book called Appalachian Ways, *I thought how the people of this area are seen as being poor, when they are really rich in their love of nature and God's creation. This log house was A. P. Carter's birthplace.*

she did. He was tall with sandy-colored hair, fair-skinned like most Carters.

How I loved Ma and Pa Carter! We went in and out all the time—me, my sister Gladys, and my brother Joe. After Mother and Daddy separated, they worried and tended to us even more. This woman, Molly Carter, was a worker. (Gladys, today, reminds me of Grandma.) I remember all the food she canned—the big jars of kraut, pickled beans, shuck beans, apples, apple butter. She made a blackberry jam that was part berries, part apples; you stirred it all day and put it in big crocks—how good it was on a biscuit! The big apple bin that hung in Ma's old dirt basement was filled with apples and pears for the winter. No one on earth made corn bread like Ma Carter. The meal was ground at Zane's Lunsford Mill. She fried streaked meat in the big fish-fry iron pan, and leaving the grease there, she crumbled the meat into her bread and then baked it in the old wood stove. Smear that with butter—man, that was good eating! Always at supper, milk and corn bread—I'd eat like a horse! She would worry, saying, "Janette, you will make a large woman; don't eat so much." It was too good not to eat it. The best breads I ever ate were Grandma's corn bread and my mother's biscuits. Then there were Grandma's apple pies, all stacked one on the other, and her molasses cake, about ten layers, all with apple butter in between. I can make the cake like Ma, but never her corn bread; maybe my meal's not as good.

Pa was very strict—you minded him! I just tagged along after Ma. How she loved flowers! They lived in a rock pile—really, it seemed more rocks than dirt. You were always moving them for flower beds. The dirt I carried—chicken litter from the barn, stump dirt from the woods—went into one big bed with a fence around it to keep out chickens. It was filled with tulips, gladiolas, every flower. The big dahlias were close to the creek. The big flower bench Pa made sat on the front porch and held all her potted plants. Flowers were everywhere. On the porch, Grandpa rocked and was grouchy, but he sat surrounded by plants! There

Myself as a baby ("Just the right size").

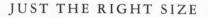

JUST THE RIGHT SIZE

Now come here, little handy one—
No doubt they're calling me.
Honor thy mom and dad, I always did believe.
The oldest one is courting; the baby he's asleep.
I am the right size; I am in between.

Chorus
Just the right size for bringing in the wood,
For milking cows and sweeping floors, I was always
*   good.*
I jumped when I was spoken to, wild cherry I despised,
Always Daddy's little doll and just the right size.

From the time I was a small child my grandma thought I was just the right size for any chore. Above, left to right, are my brother Joe, my sister Gladys, myself at the age of six, and our cousin Helen Carter. Opposite, Gladys has her arms around a friend on the left and me on the right.

Now Grandma Carter's flower beds were the talk of
    the land.
Gladiolas in a rock pile, no one could understand.
The straw, the leaves, and all debris the dirt it did
    hide.
Carried by a little girl, who's just the right size.

Chorus

Come here, little handy one — no rest I'll ever find.
Strolling by the wrong place, at just the right time.
A complete nervous wreck, the doctor he told me.
All from being overworked — the right size,
    naturally.

Chorus

was a large bed of tulips, very beautiful roses, lilies. There were huge elephant ears, and I'd try to slip off and rest under these.

I believe sincerely that Molly Carter was the working-est woman in Scott County! She never stopped saying, "You are the right size!" I was, and any grandchild who entered her yard was told the same thing. I was left there about half my childhood, so I learned to do whatever I was told! I washed dishes; I carried and dragged wood; I milked and churned; I chopped big crocks of kraut; I stirred apple butter; I stirred jam; I carried tons of dirt; I moved rocks and filled up holes with dirt, cow and chicken litter, or dry leaves. Whatever Ma said do—I did! Usually Ma rested after dinner. I'd get under the elephant ear or go wade in the cold creek. The coldest, best water in the world was there. She was a good woman—if you worked one hour, you played one hour.

My grandmother was a midwife—she delivered all three of us and half the children in Poor Valley, as well as most of her twenty-five grandchildren. You could see her with that little black satchel—and you knew when she'd come home in the early morning after worrying all night with some poor neighbor woman—well, so-and-so would have a new baby! It took me a long time to learn the meaning of this. Little girls didn't ask questions back then; you just listened and hoped when you grew up into a lady, maybe you would be told secrets, too. Grandma always said Gladys was the prettiest baby of any she ever saw.

My grandma—I trailed after her like a shadow. Every day, she'd stop and let me comb her wavy black hair, as she always said I was gentle. It was so long, she could sit on it! The tiny waves in her hair were soft as raindrops falling on her flower beds. They made me think of tiny waves of water, as when you throw a pebble in the creek and the waves go on and on. I'd brush and comb a long time, then she'd wind it all around in a large bun and cover it with a black bonnet, cover all those pretty pins and combs of hair. She was beautiful, I thought. You could see the Indian in her, in her high cheek bones and her shiny hair. Pa would sit on the porch a lot, but Ma was always on the go; from daylight until dark, she worked.

Everyone had a dammed-up place in a creek or spring house to keep milk and butter. Sometimes a storm came up, and when the water rushed down out of the mountains, milk, crocks, butter and all would go floating away! Grandma always told me to watch for snakes near the spring, which lay in the shade of a big oak. She told how Daddy (when a young boy) stepped on a copperhead there. Grandpa cut a hole in his heel, and Ma filled it with turpentine — the doctor said they saved his life!

I remember Ma's long dresses and aprons, and all those pretty white cotton petticoats. This tall, modest lady would go into the cold back room to put on her flannel gown and then come to bed with Pa by the fireplace. You'd sit on a winter night by the warm fire and watch the embers die down, then young and old would kneel on the warm hearth to listen to Pa say the evening prayer.

How they ever lived on this small farm, I don't know. They raised eight children; God helped and they depended on him! I never heard them complain. Pa was always going to tend the sick and praying, while Ma was delivering babies. They raised their food, had chickens and eggs to sell, raised tobacco and corn, and always had plenty to eat.

I remember twice talking at the table or laughing while Pa blessed the table. I was sent away, and it was almost supper before I ate. Sundays, I about starved — the old folks ate, then the preacher and company ate, and finally, at last, the small ones got to the table. I don't know, really, how I ever grew up!

Aunt Maybelle and Uncle Ezra lived next to Pa on one side, Uncle Jim and Aunt Vangie on the other side. Uncle Ezra had the biggest, prettiest home. He was a mail clerk on a train, gone a lot. Every day seemed like Sunday there. Aunt Maybelle always had a hired girl to help her with her work. Maybelle was lovely; I can see her still, playing the piano in the evening, always smiling and singing in her soft, kind voice. I loved to go play with her daughter Helen — they always had so many toys.

Being too young at the time, I cannot remember Maybelle and Eck's wedding, but they spent the night at Grandpa Carter's. They were all in bed sound asleep when all of a sudden all hell broke loose in the yard! They were shivareeing the newlyweds, with cowbells, tubs being beaten like drums, whooping and hollering. Pa came storming out in his split-tail, long-handled underwear. He was a stern man! "Go home!" he cried, jumping up and down in the night air. So they just put Pa on the greasy pole and ran around the house with him instead of Uncle Eck!

Grandpa Carter and his brother, Uncle Lish, had married sisters, Molly and Martha Bayes. Uncle Lish had strange ways. He decided one day to burn out chicken lice in the hen's nest, but he forgot that the nest was nailed to the barn. Lamp oil kills lice, but it also catches afire if it's applied to a straw nest with a match. The whole barn burned down, the hens flew off, and the cows and horses got out, but his year's supply of hay went up in black smoke.

After supper at Ma's house there were prayers. Grandpa prayed the longest prayers I ever listened to. I would stay on my knees, it seemed, one hour, but I never moved — I was afraid of Pa Carter!

My mother and her sister Mae were raised by Milburn and Melinda Nickels — Uncle Mill and Aunt Nick. Mother also had three brothers — Bob, Nathan, and Stephan Dougherty. They were all just shifted from kinfolks to friends until they were grown. I've been around my mother's people very little, but I loved these kind people. Grandpa Dougherty was a big handsome man with snow-white hair and a mustache that tickled my face when he kissed me. I used to sit on his lap, as a child. He was a great reader with a wonderful memory, studied the Bible, and was consulted by many with questions about this great book. It seemed my ancestors used the Bible as a guide.

Uncle Mill and Aunt Nick turned their home into a refuge for homeless orphans, kin, or friends. Their home was full of beds — seven beds in all. Their table was always set — when Aunt Nick finished a meal, she set the table and left the food there, and anytime anyone passed by, hungry or tired, they were welcome. No matter who! How I loved to visit them every summer. The house still stands, quiet now and filled with hay or storage.

Uncle Grant and my beautiful Aunt Theda had three children — Scotty, Benny, and Patsy. I dearly loved Uncle Grant — he was so kind. He loved to fiddle, and they said that once he went to a dance, fiddled all night until the hair fell out of the bow, and he just kept right on fiddling with the wood bow.

Then there was Uncle Jim and my bright-eyed Aunt Vangie — how I loved her! I just about stayed at their place with their daughter Lois. There was J. W., too, and Mattie Lee, Robert (my age), Juanita, Jack, and Mary Ann. No one knew the Bible like Uncle Jim. I believed he memorized it. Ask him any question, he had an answer. Uncle Ezra, Jim, and Ermine — they all studied the Bible. Uncle Ermine was our Sunday School teacher, and he was the best I ever heard. I could sit all day and listen to him and Uncle Jim teach Sunday School.

They don't make people like my people — to me, anyway. Take Aunt Vergie and Uncle Roy. Aunt Vergie reminded me of an angel. She loved everyone, helped all who needed help, gave to the poor, and raised four children — Blanche, Ruth, Esther, and R. M. Jr. She even took in homeless children. She would have fed Cox's army, if they'd gone there hungry. This beautiful lady radiated love like a sparkler. She walked in a room, and you noticed her, thinking "There is a good woman!" When she prayed it made chill bumps raise on you, to listen to her. I never saw anyone love God like her.

Uncle Howell and Aunt Sib had twin boys, Bob and Jim. My daddy was partial, I believe, to Sib. As a child he bought her this beautiful doll. It was kept in a glass case on the wall, and each year Ma made the doll a new dress and it was put up again. I use to sit and look and wish it were my doll. It had real hair, all gold like Aunt Sib's. How I wanted to play with it, but it always hung on the wall.

No one could beat Aunt Sib on a cake. I can still see her, every Saturday working over this pretty pink mixing bowl decorated with white flowers. I would stand there the whole time and watch her make the cake to get to lick the bowl. She could bake a mighty good cake. My Aunt Sib was pretty, tall and slender

These pictures were taken in Poor Valley during the 1930s. Above are Jeff and Martha Harper, the couple who rented the house in the background from us. Gladys and Joe are standing next to them, behind the old mules Kit and Maude. Below, Gladys sits between Joe and me on the boardwalk at Aunt Melinda Nichols'.

as a reed, with her golden hair and blue eyes. Those tiny hands could play an autoharp, and she could sing tenor like no one I ever heard.

They were proud, my people. They worked so hard—they shared their food, their love, their lives. All the neighbors were intertwined. They helped one another in sickness—or in a season of plenty. Neighbors were close to one another. They all worked to survive! If our cow went dry, some neighbor had one with a new calf. They shared the milk, fruit, gardens. When a neighbor died, the men dug a grave with a pick and shovel. As a child I thought the most horrible sound on earth was dirt clods hitting the casket after it had been lowered into the ground. I would cling to my daddy's hand and thank God I still had my parents! And tears would fall. My heart ached for those who had died and left children and family.

The old dirt road was dusty in summer, icy in the cold winter. Once Daddy poured us a concrete front porch. It was his pride. He went to bed thinking it would be dry and set by morning. He awoke to hear wheels running to and fro on the porch. Little Joe was riding his tricycle, saying, "I'm making ruts, Daddy, so it will look like the road."

Myself, I find it hard to write about.

Mother said I wasn't pretty like Joe and Gladys, and I was certainly no beauty as a child. My mother once laughingly said, "Janette was the ugliest baby I ever saw." My daddy said, "To me, she was pretty." But then I always felt I was Daddy's pet. I was in the middle, neither a baby nor a beauty. I always worried because I only had one name. I always wanted love—not that I was unloved, but I felt love kept mothers and daddies together, and then mine separated. That's a child's view—it took me years to find you do what you feel best with your life.

I loved to pick blackberries, huckleberries, dewberries, any berry—to get out of the fields! I was tanned a dark brown, almost black as a walnut, from Poor Valley's sunshine—my hair bleached snow white. I wished I had black wavy hair like my mother. Mine was straight as a stick and always cut very short. I did have brown eyes, though never beautiful like hers. I was called Blackie!

Farm work was dirty work — plowing the fields of corn and tobacco with two old mules. I didn't like to hoe all day in the hot sun, but I did. I was always glad to get home at the close of day to eat supper and see my mother.

It seems I did a lot of dishes. That was my job — no one else's, it seemed! I was so small that I stood in a chair to do them. One of my spankings was over dishes. "I am tired of dishes. I'm not going to wash no more," I said. My little legs carried stripes for a week. I never spoke again of dishes, just automatically washed all I found dirty from then on. Today, one of my most cherished possessions is a dishwasher, a gift from a friend, Mary Ann.

Never do I remember my mother spanking me. Her voice was always so kind, so calm. Daddy had a violent temper. I felt, if she said, "Punish Janette," he would. He always listened to mother, and he always used a razor strap, if not a wild cherry switch. Next door, where Ben and Myrtle lived, stood one of the largest wild cherry trees I ever saw! It had hundreds of switches, and they stung like yellowjackets. I used to wish all those old trees would be sawed up into firewood!

Three times is all my daddy whipped me, but they were enough to make a believer out of me — I obeyed him! The first time was over the dishes; the second time, Joe and I were fighting, just like cats and dogs. He was pulling my hair; his was too short to pull. We both were well punished. That was our first and only fight in our whole life.

When I was fourteen years old, a young lady, I received my last punishment. I begged to spend the night with Louise. Daddy said no. Well, I disobeyed! When the bus passed our house, I never got off — I just kept going! I knew the next day, after school, Daddy would be sitting on the porch waiting, with that long switch looking more like a young tree across his lap. I still remember the blue print dress I was wearing and how I kept thinking, "I hope it don't tear from the switch." It's hard to stand when you are grown and take punishment, but I stood, and when I looked there were tears in Daddy's eyes. He was thinking, "You have to learn to obey." It hurt him to hurt me, but I was stubborn!

We didn't have much money — no one in Poor Valley did. You lived off what you raised in the garden. Most everyone had a mule, a cow, hogs and chickens. Daddy once bought me a little bantam rooster and a hen. How I loved an old setting hen and to have more little chickens! But I didn't like to carry the old squalling hens to the store. You carried the hens, roosters, or eggs to Neal's Store about a mile away and traded them for groceries. It was all right, though — you could get a sucker or a box of Cracker Jacks for your trouble and get out of the corn field, too, if it was summer.

There was food cooked by my mother's hands — she's the world's best. I can still taste her tomato gravy and biscuits, chicken and dumplings on a Sunday, the fresh berries we picked for the pies in the spring, the cold milk and corn bread around the kitchen table on a winter night. No one ate until Daddy asked the blessing — "Thank you, God, for these and all other blessings — pardon and forgive our sins and in Heaven, save us! Amen."

Mount Vernon Church was built by people in the Valley. There's three generations of Carters buried there. Everyone went to church — there was a long line of friends, walking, every Sunday. There was singing, preaching, praying, shouting — they would shout clear out the door. I saw one lady go out the door and disappear down the gap, shouting. She went clear on home, praising God!

The preacher always ate dinner with somebody. A lot of times it was at Grandma's — the word had got out about her fried chicken and corn bread. She could cook! She was well known for her cakes and biscuits. Sunday cakes had icings, but the ones through the week were plain and baked in a skillet. I liked them;

Aunt Melinda and Uncle Milburn Nichols, who raised my mother from the age of two.

you ate them like you would a piece of bread — just break off a hunk and go sit under an elephant ear plant.

Sunday School was where you went on Sunday morning to listen to Mrs. Dennison teach about Jesus and to give a penny for the little card you kept. Then the preacher preached (I would get so hungry and tired before all this was over), but you were very quiet through it all. You sat still while the older people shouted. To me, the church was always so quiet and peaceful, nestled down among tall pines, on a hill away from the road. I loved to hear Uncle Fland Bayes lead the singing. He was my great-uncle, and he and Aunt Etter had twelve children. He taught singing school all over the county. The church was always full. It is still, to me, a sacred, precious spot. I found Jesus in this valley, and I want to be buried here. I want to rest here — where the wind blows through the tall pines, overlooking the valley where I roamed as a child and the hills and mountains that I climbed, dragging out wood over the road to Grandma's house when the snow was a blanket of white.

A six-week-old baby doesn't remember, but I've been told my mother almost died in an accident. When she and Gladys and I were riding from Grandma's, the horse got scared and ran away with the buggy. My mother was dragged; I was thrown clear and landed in Dicey Thomas's rose bush, while Gladys landed in the big road. For a long time, my mother was very sick. She couldn't even let me nurse, and so Dicey took over. I scooted her daughter Loraine over; she shared her mother with me. We all loved Dicey Thomas. She had a houseful — seven children — but she kept us a lot, too. She tended to me for six weeks.

One year the creek overflowed into a meadow back of the house filled with tall trees. It was wet and cold — like early springs always are. Daddy decided to sell those trees for paper wood. They had to be sawed down with a crosscut saw, and all the bark had to be peeled off them before the ground could be cleared off to later be turned into another corn field! Joe and I did all we could do. All day I pulled bark; my hands hurt and my head throbbed. I kept saying I was sick. Daddy said, "You are lazy." I tried to walk, but I was reeling like a Poor Valley drunk. I vomited up green water; I even turned green. No doubt, I'd done about all I could do, so I was carried into the house in Daddy's strong arms. Mother came, as she always did if you were very sick, and I was very sick for three days. I tried to get out of bed, but I kept reeling, so I was nursed back to health by my mother's hands. The best medicine on earth was the feel of her soft hands. She could play a guitar and wipe away tears, oh so gently. She would sing to try to calm me down. Then she decided I needed a tonic! "She's run down; she needs iron," Doc said. "Go get her wine of cardui." Have you ever drunk that awful stuff? Castor oil tasted good by comparison.

"Get Lois some," Aunt Vangie said. "She looks pale." If I looked pale, Lois did, too.

That spring I was "built-up." It was an awful time—my stomach was torn all to whiz.

At Maces Springs School you caught all diseases—chicken pox, lice, itch, whooping cough, colds. Everytime I got sick, Joe did. We had measles, the worst kind, and we were put in the same bed. Mother was sent for, again. I felt sure I was going blind—my eyes looked like two fried eggs in a mud hole. There were quilts over the windows, making the room dark as a dungeon. For five days all I saw of daylight was my mother coming through the door with another cup of hot sassafras tea. I was hot; Joe was hot as a pod of hot pepper. With every cup of hot tea, I got sicker and redder. I prayed for something cold to drink, but it had to be hot to break the measles out. I felt Joe and I would both go up in a blue blaze amid straw ticks, featherbeds and all. It was awful!

Only once in my life did they send for old Doctor Meade who lived at Mendota. That once it was beyond my mother's, daddy's, and grandma's knowledge of just what to do. I had dragged wood at Grandma's all day long and stopped at Aunt Maybelle's on my

These two old buildings bring back memories. Some of my people were born in the log house. The scene of the old sawmill shows the Nob, where we so often played.

way home. She didn't put you to work like most relations. My neck was hurting every time I turned my head. I screamed with pain, and Maybelle put me in her big clean bed. I was looked at and discussed by my elders and introduced to a new medicine, while waiting for the doctor to come on the scene—I was drenched and rubbed down with turpentine! This was worse than sunburn, and I only screamed louder. No doubt, Dr. Meade saved my life—I was given a shot to calm me, sponged off with ice water, rubbed with something besides Vicks salve and given (for once) a good-tasting medicine. How I ever grew up is a mystery to me—but I made it!

Old cows never came home to be milked. In the late evening, you had to hunt in meadows, dark hollows—I would listen for the cow bells, then run and use a stick to warp those old stubborn cows. They were always hunting greener grass away from the barn. Instead of gates, there were poles to take up and down for the cows to go from one pasture to another. There was lots of barbed wire near these, and I still carry a scar where, instead of taking them down, I climbed them (saving time), jumped to the ground, and forgot to turn my arms loose. Circling the post, I felt a blinding pain, and to my horror, a big piece of flesh from a hole in my arm hung on the wire. I was screaming for Ma to do something, crying, "Where's your black satchel; can't you sew it back?" Daddy and Mother were gone. Ma told Pa, "It needs stitches, but I'll fix it." Ma always did fix things. She crammed it full of hog lard and dry sulphur; but I whimpered, "I want my own skin there."

"Just leave it," she said. "The blackbirds will eat it." I watched birds several days, looking for the piece of my arm!

My first husband first saw me when I was all of eight years old, driving cows with Daddy to Mr. Jett's land to pasture them. He was eighteen years old. He never dreamed he'd marry the barefoot girl who chased old cows; he courted all the girls in Poor Valley until I grew up.

I was tall, skinny, gawky, shy. For the most part, I just followed around behind someone, and I studied. I tried very hard to learn, and I did learn! I got a medal for scholarship, a new dress, and my daddy came to see me make my speech. He'd bought my dress, too — it was white and very pretty. I spent a lot of hours studying. When all the others had gone to bed, there was just me, the oil lamp, and the kitchen table!

I don't guess any child has loved their parents more than I did. Their fame never entered my mind — I loved them because they were my own mother and daddy. After they got into the music business there was more to eat, it seemed, more money, and we bought a car. But our cars were never in too good a shape! I remember flats, always flats. Or sometimes the car just stopped, and Daddy said, "Janette, get out and push." I always tried to do whatever I was told to do, but pushing a car isn't easy for a small girl. I spent a lot of time pushing.

Once, when Daddy was gone on a trip in our car, Mother was sweeping the front porch. There was an awful commotion coming up the valley road, and I can still see the shocked look on her face, the broom stopped in mid air. "That Doc [Daddy] is dragging a sawmill up the road with our car!" she exclaimed. He'd done just that — dragged it many miles. Big trucks and trains usually pulled sawmills, but A. P. Carter pulled his own sawmill home. He sure kept Poor Valley in an uproar, and Mother never knew "What next?"

Even with the car, you walked a lot. I remember several times walking across Clinch Mountain to visit Aunt Nick. It's beautiful, but quite a mountain for a little girl to climb. I can also remember every fall riding the train that ran by the house into Bristol, Virginia. Mother took all three of us to buy school clothes, and we'd stay all night at a hotel, eating hot dogs for dinner. Back then you didn't go to town; you didn't get toys and candy, except at Christmas. Every year for school we got a toboggan, brown gloves, brown galoshes, a sweater, maybe a coat (I usually got Gladys's old one; she got the new one), cotton socks, a new pair of shoes (you went barefoot all summer), and a dress or two for Sunday. I'd pick huckleberries and sell them to buy material for Mother or Myrtle Hensley to make me dresses for school. Lois and I would trail behind Fred, Myrtle's son. He'd kill snakes and find patches of berries. We'd climb trees and wade through the little streams of water flowing down the mountain into the creeks that fed old Holston.

I found out early the meaning of the word "stealing." No one had told me about it, but I found out! I loved Myrtle Hensley. We were in and out of her house, and Fred was my friend. He didn't chase me with snakes or bugs, like Joe did. He held my hand when we walked to school. There was a woodbox back of her cooking stove and in it one day there lay a pretty box with a red rose on top. I just picked it up and took it home! Gladys wore me out with wild cherry when she found out. My legs were switched all the way to Myrtle's house, with Gladys saying, "Tell her you are sorry." Well, I told her! She gave me the box — it was only there to build a fire. But I'd stolen something. From then on, I asked!

I went everywhere my daddy did — I'd walk all day, ride a car, go out collecting songs; anywhere he went, I tried to go. One night he took me to a revival meeting, and the best thing that ever happened in my life happened that night. I found Jesus! I was saved, and I joined the Mount Vernon Church. I was baptized at the age of thirteen — my sins washed away in Holston River, down at Ethel Owens's where the river was just the right depth for baptizing. Gladys, Joe, and I were all baptized the same Sunday. I can still see my Grandma shouting and feel my daddy's arms holding me close, while tears ran down his face onto my wet hair. That was the best feeling I ever had — when I found a friend, my Jesus! I had always felt I was alone, even when surrounded by my family and friends. But from that day on, He's never left me. He listens to my prayers, my needs, my mistakes — I tell Him everything! Before that day, my closest friend was Daddy, but he and Mother always said, "Believe in God." I had never fully understood what that meant, but on that day I found out why

I'VE FOUND JESUS

For years I've been searching for a love
    that is real,
For someone who cares just for me,
A Savior to help me, no matter what comes,
I've found Jesus, you see.

Chorus
I've found someone, someone who's real,
A peace that is restful and free,
A Savior to help me, no matter what comes,
I've found Jesus, you see.

Many times I will stumble,
Many times I will fall.
There's someone standing by me,
To reach out and help me by lending His hand.
Dear child, dear child, follow me!

Chorus

The Lord is my Shepherd; I shall not want.
My every need He'll supply.
He'll go with me, through valleys of death.
In Heaven with Him, I'll abide.

Chorus

At thirteen I was baptized and joined the Mount Vernon Church. Above, I'm pictured with my mother Sara. That was a happy time for me!

people shouted, why you love all people, even those who mistreat you. I found peace! My life has been as rocky as the rocks in Grandma's yard, but I know I can pray, any minute, day or night, and He listens to me. I wander back to the mountain, and I just tell Him everything! It's a secret He and I have — no one knows how often we talk. I pray everywhere — walking on a stage, looking out at hundreds of people. I'm no musician; I'm not even much of a singer, but God thinks I'm all right. I belong to Him! He's stood by even when my heart was broken like a shattered china plate. I'd give up my mother, my daddy, my Aunt Maybelle (I loved her like a mother, too). I've felt I would surely die, I could not sing or go on, but a voice said, "I'll go with you." So there's my Jesus again — always there!

When I was fifteen, I was jerked up and taken to Del Rio, Texas. My parents were there working with Maybelle, Helen, June, and Anita. They were being heard singing from XERA, a large radio station in Villa Acuna, Mexico, right across the border from Texas, and they were making transcriptions. I took Joe with me, and he, Daddy, and I lived in a little house. Mother had married Coy Bayes by then, and they lived in an apartment. I hated Texas with a purple passion; I cried for one whole year. I hated the big city, and the hot deserts with no shade trees. I was so homesick, I almost cried my eyes out. I made twenty dollars a week, and I started saving money to come home at Christmas. I bought my clothes and sang when I was told to. I missed my schoolmates, Poor Valley, Grandma Carter, and most of all I was in love. I came home the next year and married. I have always been a very determined person and have done things against my elders' advice! But I was young and very stubborn then.

A. P. and Sara Carter

I've heard my daddy tell over and over again how he met Sara Elizabeth Dougherty. He was selling fruit trees and stopped at the farm of Mr. Milburn Nickels in Midway, Virginia. He heard a beautiful voice singing "Engine 143" — a voice he could hear clear and sweet even before he got into the yard. She was playing an autoharp.

He used to say, "She was the most beautiful girl I ever saw." Her brown eyes — never has anyone had eyes like my mother — seemed to have gold stars and shone like diamonds. He loved her long, wavy black hair. When she cut her hair years later, my daddy tied it with a red ribbon. Joe has it now, kept in a trunk. How he loved her, this sixteen-year-old girl. She was like a beautiful painting — you had to see her and know her to know there was such beauty. She always reminded me of an Indian maiden or a queen. If you ever met her, you never forgot her! So my daddy kept walking back and forth across Clinch Mountain until he won her heart. They were married when she was just sixteen, and they moved to Maces Springs, in the valley.

Hard labor was Daddy and Mother's life — I've heard neighbors speak of her, working by his side, dragging trees out of the mountain with the help of our mules, Kit and Maude, to saw them into crossties. No doubt some of the ties on the railroad were the result of their struggles.

As I've grown older and had children of my own, I've thought a lot about my mother's childhood. She was orphaned as a child of three. To never know a mother seems terrible. All she had of her mother was a picture. There was a poet who wrote that Jesus was God's only begotten Son; He gave Him up to die for the sins of the world, and so to fill in — He gave us mothers! But Sara and her sister Mae were raised by Mill and Melinda Nickels, their mother's sister. Grandpa Dougherty had three boys, too, but they were all scattered to and fro until they grew up.

I never in all my life heard Sara Carter speak unkindly of anyone. She loved people. This gentle lady would give you the coat off her back. No wonder my daddy loved my mother! I look at her from a child's point of view, but all the fans who ever met her said, "She is a beautiful woman."

Gladys and I always seemed pale compared to her. Mother, to me, was always as beautiful as she was when I was small, right up to the day she died, on January 8, 1979. Her hands were always a musician's hands that could stroke an autoharp or wipe away my tears, oh, so gently! Her soft voice was very calm and easygoing. She was always so kind, giving me her pretty clothes, trying to help me, and worrying over all her children — like all mothers do.

My mother ran her home like clockwork. I knew as sure as my feet hit the floor, I would be washed all over and scrubbed clean from my hair to my toes with old lye soap. I felt like everything smelled of lye — my hair, clothes, skin. I wished I could use my mother's perfume; it was in a little dispenser on her dresser. Her skin, her clothes, and her hair always smelled like a wild rose that grew in the fields where I picked dewberries.

I can still feel the touch of her clean beds — the sheets as white as the driven snow that blew around our house in the cold

SARA LEE

The path through the woods, from your
    house to mine,
I wandered one day, not knowing I'd find
An angel who sings like birds in the trees,
I found my Sara Lee.

Chorus
I'd give you the world, try very hard.
I'll plant roses in your back yard.
My life, my love, I gave to thee,
My dearest, my Sara Lee.

Sparkling rain drops fall on your hair
Like dark, rippling waves — my darling I care.
Stars in your eyes, shining for me —
I worshiped my Sara Lee.

Chorus

I wrote this song about the days when my daddy courted my beautiful mother Sara (above). Below, A. P. Carter as a young man.

Roses are gone, leaves turning brown,
Winter winds blow, snow covers the ground.
The last golden sunset, I walk alone.
Very soon, my dear, I'll be gone!

Chorus

winter. I can still smell her ham meat, tomato gravy, and blackberry pie. On Sundays there was chicken and dumplings. Always when we picked blackberries, we could go swim in the Holston River to wash away old chiggers. I would gladly pick berries all day to go swimming! Everything about her was neat and clean. A grass sack, if she'd worn one, would have been clean.

There has never been or ever will be a voice like my mother's. I remember when I was a child and sick with the measles she said, "What can I do, or do you want something?" I told her to sing and she would. That was the best medicine — my mother's singing.

The biggest compliment I ever get is, "You favor Sara" or "You sing like her." There's no comparison! I'm willing to just walk in the shadows of her and my daddy.

Daddy, christened Alvin Pleasant Delaney Carter, was the oldest child of Robert and Molly Carter. After him came James, Ezra and Virgie (twins), Ettaleen, Grant, Ermine, and Sylvia. But I always thought Grandma Carter loved Daddy most of all.

Gladys always seemed to be Mother's pride — she and Joe. I always felt I was Daddy's little girl. I cried to go everywhere he'd go. I would cling to his hand, walk until my legs gave out, and then he'd carry me. He was so very handsome — tall, with wavy black hair and the kindest blue eyes like the sky on a clear sunny day. I remember going to visit Ma and Pa Carter, coming home in the twilight. Mother carried Joe, Daddy carried me, and Gladys skipped along behind.

My daddy had a quick temper, but I was never afraid of him. I knew if I obeyed, I wouldn't get a whipping, and I tried very hard to obey! I could always talk to Daddy; he was a very understanding person. I spent many hours walking behind this giant of a man. There is a saying, "Any man can become a father, but very few are Daddies." To walk close by him and hold his trembling hand was the greatest thrill. I'd go anywhere to be near him.

It seemed to me my daddy was a lonely man but, with his

beautiful smile, a kind man. I remember him as always trying to help others less fortunate than he. On the little valley farm, the three small tenant houses were rented to farmers whom he helped more than they helped him. He was an honest man, and we were taught honesty at a very early age — you just didn't lie to Daddy.

Grandma claimed he was marked. Before he was born lightning struck a tree where she was gathering apples, and fire ran all on the ground and scared her; so Daddy was born nervous. He always was nervous — I remember his trembling hands as he reached out to hold my little hand or stroke my hair.

Daddy had very little schooling. His writing was poor due to his hands trembling. Children laughed at him, so he was taken out of school at a very early age. He loved books, though, and to travel and meet people in his search for songs or sketches of tunes, phrases, etc. I would tag along, as I could memorize well. I loved to hear him sing or hum a tune as he went about his work, never realizing (I don't guess) that he was singing. Later, with the "Carter Family," his deep bass voice was always wandering off when he should have been standing still, while Mother and Maybelle practiced for a recording session. He often seemed to me to be in deep study; I guess he was trying to write a song.

He loved land; his money was invested in land. I know he worked long years and hard for this investment. He left land and a house to each child. I don't believe his mind was ever off his children — Gladys, Joe, and me. He never made a difference, loved all three equally.

Daddy was a Christian man and had deep faith in God. He read the Bible a lot, yet he didn't go around talking Christianity all the time. He showed his feelings by his kindness to others. He never met anyone he felt was a stranger; if you stopped, you ate or spent the night. Though we lived very simply, we never felt poor; there were Mother and Daddy to look after you, and all kinds of relations to love you.

"My Little Home at the Foot of Clinch Mountain" was what Daddy wrote about when he was a young man in his twenties. It was when he went out in the world to seek a fortune and to work, and was riding a train to Indiana, that he felt homesick and wrote "My Clinch Mountain Home." He almost died on that trip; he arrived home with typhoid fever and lay near death a long time, nursed by his mother.

He was a restless man, Mother said. When Gladys was being born, he walked to Mendota, Virginia (eight miles away) to get a doctor, and she was already born when he got home at daylight. Grandma was there, of course. Four years later I was born with only Grandma to help Mother; Daddy was gone. He was home when Joe was born, though, with poor Ma seeing yet another grandchild.

Daddy always walked up and down the railroad tracks, his hands behind his back. My son Dale is so like him — walks all the time, too. Never still, quick-tempered, but so gentle and kind. Everyone loved Daddy, and everybody loves my Dale. He's named for him — James Delaney Jett. Daddy worried over Dale, who was just three when Daddy died in 1960. He told me, "Be kind to him, as he has a high portion in nerves, and he will have it hard in life." He would scare me half to death, Dale — he would hold his breath and pass out cold. Daddy said he had a temper; he would faint until he cooled off, then come to.

Daddy was a man who had more than one idea in his mind. A dreamer, I suppose, but he had a way of getting what he wanted done. He would keep talking and walking till you'd just give in to him in despair. Daddy had long legs. I remember once I was so tired, I cried, so I was carried until I rested. Then, at the top of the mountain, we sat beneath a big oak and looked down on the other side. He was so strong, too. I heard a neighbor tell once how a tree was cut, and three men tried to lift one end but they couldn't — so Daddy just picked up the whole tree!

A. P. Carter had an unbelievable voice. His range was high or low; he could find all scales and chords. He sang when he felt like singing. It was no practiced effort; he just sang every now and then. He would walk to and fro, even on stage. He drove my mother and Maybelle up a wall!

CLOSE OF A DAY

In visions I see children laughing,
The weeds in the corn, hoed away.
To walk in the dust of a man you could trust —
His earnings were earned the hard way.
To rest in the cool of the evening —
The works all done; now you may play.
A mother's sweet kiss, things I often miss
Are gone like the close of a day.

This song is about my mother, my daddy, and my childhood. The photo above, taken at my first outside show at the old store, shows Poor Valley at night; I'm up on the stage.

Chorus
I'm nearing the end of a beautiful day.
My worries like sunsets, they fade away.
To kneel 'round the hearth with loved ones and pray.
At the close of a day.

The trials of life, I learned early,
To humbly pray and rely
Though skies may be grey, to trust and obey
A power much greater than I.

Chorus

And when the last mile I have traveled
My faltering steps no longer sway.
The last rays of sun shining warm on my hands,
I'll rest at the close of a day.

Chorus

A strange man at times, he would start jobs, go on to another, and not finish what he started—to my mother's dismay. Mother spend her time telling him, "Doc, change clothes," "Pick up your tools." When Daddy finished a job, he never cleaned up; someone else did, while he just calmly walked off! He would start a job then walk off till he took a notion to come back and finish what he'd started. It might be a month later. Talking about it only upset him—they were as different as night and day, my parents.

Mother and Daddy separated when we were all very small. Most of the time we were in Daddy's care—sometimes with Grandma Carter and sometimes with Mother. We still had a lot of chores to do and had to go to school, too. Gladys Ettaleen was the oldest, and she became more of a mother to me and my brother Joe Sevier. My memory of that time is being alone and looking out for myself. Daddy was gone a lot! He followed several trades— a farmer, a carpenter, a salesman; he owned a sawmill, a grist mill, a grocery store; he wrote songs and collected them, too. He worked on one job, then another.

After they separated, Mother lived with Aunt Nick and Uncle Mill. I would watch the train coming to see if my mother was on it. If so, she waved and I ran as fast as my legs could go, to be loved by my beautiful mother. When in the valley, she stayed at Maybelle's. If we got real sick, she would come and take care of us.

In the summer we were left at Aunt Nick and Uncle Mill's a few days, and once I remember going at Christmas. I can still see Daddy walking away through the fields—alone. My heart broke. I started running and crying, "I want to go with you!" So he took my hand, and we spent that Christmas together in Poor Valley.

Music meant my mother and daddy together. When there was music and singing there was no quarreling. I felt that through "music" I was surrounded by love.

When the Carter Family broke up in the forties, my daddy changed. He seemed lonelier, he walked more, and his laughing blue eyes seemed sad. His life was music. He loved that and tried the hardest of any man I ever knew to keep music alive. He was getting old, he was tired, and his health was failing. When he would sit on the porch to sing and play the guitar, I'd go sit close by and tears would come to my eyes — I'd choke up. He gave so much to the world, and I felt he never got a lot in return. When he died on November 7, 1960, I felt I would surely die, too. How could I go on? He was my dearest friend, and when he was gone I felt I was the loneliest person in the world.

Daddy is buried at Mount Vernon Church Cemetery, where his mother and daddy are laid to rest. There is no need for me to dwell on his passing away. Only God knows how much I loved him — how much I miss him. I lost the best friend I ever had, next to God. I could always talk to him. He was there to turn to when I had trials in life, and I had more than my share. He was a man who loved only one woman — my beautiful mother. I feel his presence every day in his songs; I hear them sung by others. I walk in the fields where he walked or sing in the store he built with his own two hands. His teachings of God will never leave me. I still wish I could feel his hand or see him smile. My consolation is this: Someday, I will see him again!

A big black cloud blocked out my sunlight on those darkest days when a terrible black hearse brought first my daddy, then my mother up the valley! I wanted to scream; I wanted to run. My heart was breaking like tiny fragments of glass, like a shattered china plate falling around my feet. I felt I would choke to death with the tears falling like raindrops on Grandma's flower bed, but I just stood and looked out the window where I had looked all my life for my mommy and daddy. A part of me died on those two awful days. The cold winter winds blowing were no colder than I was — I felt I would be numb the rest of my life. I'm proud to be the daughter of those famous people, but most of all I'm proud I was loved. I can feel that love so very deeply. They sowed the wheat; I'm reaping the harvest! With every check that comes from their work, I feel guilty — I don't want their money; I want them! By just being my mother and daddy, they gave to me the greatest gift. I'll go on; I promised my daddy, "I will try."

Above are Gladys, Joe, and myself at fourteen during the 1930s, in the yard where we grew up, and Joe standing next to the old gate. Below, Joe practicing his shooting next to the hollyhocks near our house. These pictures bring tears to my eyes!

Gladys and Joe

My sister is known to most everyone as G. G., the name given her by her grandchildren — Dewanna Flo, Yolanda Sue, Mark Eugene, and Dana Ettaleen. She has one daughter, Nancy Flo, and had a baby, Carolyn Beth, who died at five months. When I speak of G. G. it's hard to tell in words how much she means to me. She's four years older than I am and more like a mother. To me she favors Daddy with her dark hair and blue eyes. Others say she favors Aunt Maybelle. Never have I seen a woman like her. She can work circles around me — she can sew, she can farm, she will try anything. She's plain spoken, telling you exactly what she thinks of you right then and there — in all, a very lovely person.

I've always envied her husband, but I'm glad he's my brother-in-law. They never made a man like Milan Millard, the best man on earth. If all women had a husband like Milan! He's always treated me like a sister, and I'm sure he loves me as much as Joe does.

Joe and I were left in G. G.'s care a lot when Daddy, Mother, and Maybelle were on the road. She had so much work to do,

Gladys did. The times she used wild cherry on me, I didn't feel I needed it, but I suppose I did. Anyway, I got it! Joe was into everything, and she carried him, spanked him, loved him — that "Joe Bull" was something. Through all the hard times growing up, she was there to watch over me and Joe like a mother hen. She should have an award for baby-sitting! Her voice was very soft and clear; she could sing but never did. I think of the dresses she's made me, the advice, the tears — and through all my trials she's stood by like the rock of Gibraltar. We've always been very close and loved one another. It seemed we were closer to each other than were the cousins who always had mothers and daddies on hand.

I remember the time I got lost from Gladys at Mendota's first medicine show. We all went in Steve and Myrtle's wagon, pulled by a team of mules — a wagonful of people. Sometime during the show Gladys left with Milan Millard, who was her sweetheart then. I was forgotten, I suppose! Anyway, I cried all the way home to Myrtle's, wanting Gladys. She found me there the next day.

Gladys was the one who tended Joe while the Carter Family auditioned for Ralph Peer. Joe disturbed all Bristol with his crying. He was nine months old, a fat, pretty baby, and he wanted to nurse, but his mother was singing. So he was fed ice cream, something he hadn't had. I guess his stomach hurt; anyway, Gladys said she got very tired of hearing him cry. I wasn't there; I was left at Grandma Carter's to wait out that eventful day.

Nancy Flo, G. G.'s daughter, is very special to me. She was my first niece, so she's closer. She's the best little mother; I see her and Johnny, her husband, going to church every Sunday with their four pretty children.

G. G. and Milan have a beautiful home. I guess it's Poor Valley's hotel — so many people have eaten and slept there. There are a lot of Carters and relations. She has bedrooms and beds for company, a large rambling house. They remind me of Uncle Mill and Aunt Nick with the kindness they show to all who come to visit the home of the Carter Family.

Daddy said Gladys would cry for the moon, and he used to

tell her, "You can't have that." Ma Carter said, too, that she was the prettiest baby she ever saw. I wonder how one woman can do so much work; when she starts something, she hangs right on. I give out, have to rest, but from daylight to dark she works like fighting fire. Uncle Grant always said, "One day she'll fold up like an accordion." She is something, though, my G. G.!

My brother (Uncle Ezra called him Joe Bull), I remember as a very pretty baby with his big blue eyes, blonde curls, and the little checkered aprons, dresses with buttons up the back, that Mother made for him in red, yellow, green, all colors. How he loved Gladys! She could rock him and hold him when no one else could. They never made a more mischievous little boy.

I barely remember the small two-room house where Joe was born on February 27, 1927. I didn't like him! I climbed on the bed and looked at this pretty baby, tugging at my mother's breast, and tears ran down my cheeks. I said, "I'm not the baby anymore," and I heard my mother say, "I have two babies now." I soon loved Joe; everyone loved him. Gladys was his second mother, if Mother was gone to record or sing. He was rocked, petted, and carried. I never saw one little boy get so much attention. He demanded attention! Most of my life was spent hunting Joe. He kept the dust all stirred up in Poor Valley.

He was our valley's first streaker. Just like Daddy shucked corn, Joe got rid of his clothes. He'd take them all off — evidently he hated them! I can still see him running like a blue streak up the road with Gladys or me right behind, the old train whistle blowing and the engineer laughing at this unusual scene. He ran through creeks and wheatfields; he'd crawl under the house and hide for hours on end.

Houses weren't underpinned where I grew up. Chickens and dogs slept under the house, and Joe had a way of going under the house, as far back as he could possibly get, naked as a picked bird. "Go get him," someone would say. Well, I worried off and on for one whole day, but every time I about got near enough to drag him out, I was hit in the face with dirt or chicken litter! He finally crawled out from sheer hunger. He was spanked by mother. He was always being spanked, then loved. He was one mischievous small boy!

Neal's store was a place where the neighbors gathered to talk of crops, gossip, buy groceries, and watch the train go by. One day all the people in Poor Valley were gathered there with the children herded up like sheep! A doctor was there to vaccinate all the school children against smallpox. "Surely Daddy won't let this ugly man stick that long needle in my arm!" we said to ourselves. Gladys had gone through this ordeal calmly. I was picked up and held in Daddy's arms, and then I was stabbed! I cried and held on for dear life. "Where's Joe?" they asked then. "He's next." So there I went, under another strange building—I'd worn a path under ours—and I could feel myself crawling on a snake, but I found him.

I'd had my experience with snakes! They scared me within an inch of my life. Joe whipped my bare legs with one once—a dead one, thank God! I ran for a half-mile, screaming and showing the bottoms of my feet. That was the fastest I ever ran in my whole life! I was scared to death. To this day, at the sight of a snake, dead or alive, I almost faint!

Joe sat and pondered mean things to do. He'd gather frogs, tadpoles, bugs, spiders, or worms and scare me. As for me, I loved cats, all cats. I dragged them home. I hunted poor, sick, sore-eyed cats that no one wanted and that had been thrown along the river or county roads. I'd slip them in my bed (I slept upstairs) because it was winter and cold! I'd pray they wouldn't whine or purr, but they would—and then wham! Gladys threw them out the window, and I'd cry myself to sleep, thinking surely the cat would be in a dead heap the next morning. But there it would sit at the door, wanting gravy. I loved gravy on a biscuit—that was good eating—and I always took out too much so that my cat could eat, too. Gladys, I suppose only thinking of my health, finally said, "Drown them, Joe." Have you ever stood on a creek bank and watched your pet being drowned? Joe was one mean little boy. I'd dig graves for the cats, pick daisies, make tombstones out of little rocks—I had a cemetery!

When Joe was all of three years old, he, Helen, and Juanita slipped off to the top of Clinch Mountain. I'm quite sure this was Joe Bull's idea! My poor mother and Maybelle's crying turned into hysterical screaming! I knew Daddy's blood pressure was rising when he started turning red and shaking like a leaf. Uncle Eck was angry, too—he was almost pawing the ground, he was so upset. I ran through the fields. I plunged into briar patches. I looked under all the houses up and down the road. I went through the culverts the train ran over, looking for them. The neighbors dragged wells—the whole valley was hunting for these lost children. I had run and cried till I was on the verge of collapse. It was almost dark when they were found at the top of Clinch. Joe's bottom end was soon torn up like a new ground—Daddy whipped him good! The little girls just followed Joe, they said, so they weren't spanked. Helen was all scratches and hurt enough already. Joe, the oldest of the three, had just decided there was another side to old Clinch!

Joe loved to kill tobacco worms. I remember Daddy taking us to worm and sucker tobacco. It was no use to say "I'll get sick," though I always did—you did as you were told. I remember the smell of green tobacco and the old worms I'd gather in tin cans for Joe. He'd gladly sit under a shade tree and mash them with rocks. Then one day it dawned on me that I was doing all the work, while Joe was resting! Daddy had left—he had a bad habit of placing you on a job and disappearing. So I got me a little switch, thinking Gladys made Joe mind, why couldn't I? I started toward him, but wham! I was hit between the eyes with a very hard green papaw. I just collapsed; what with the old worms, the hot sun, and the smell of green tobacco, it was more than I could take to be hit on the head by Joe. He revived me with cold water; he was all shook up. That one day he helped finish the job, and I got to sit in the shade while he pulled worms. I never spanked Joe, though he needed it; I always watched over him and loved him.

Every spring Grandma Carter "set" the old hens to hatch.

IF ONLY I WERE A CHILD AGAIN

Another spring, another year has vanished.
All too soon, I realize I'm old!
The tender years of life I took for granted
Are memories, more precious now than gold.
Dew drops sparkling in the morning sunlight,
Warm winds blow o'er fields of golden grain,
To hear my father praying in the twilight,
If only I were a child, again!

To see the dog woods blooming on the hillside,
The grassy moss beside a mountain stream,
The feel of brown earth, sifting through my fingers,
If only I were a child again!

A Sunday walk, a family undivided,
A country church beside a wooded lane,
Relations, friends, all singing, praising Jesus,
If only I were a child, again.

*I keep thinking back on my childhood days, and I know I am
growing old. Opposite, Gladys in the 1920s with Cecil Hensley,
who lived next door. Below, class at Maces Springs School. Joe is in
the front row, on the far left; I'm in the back somewhere.*

Soon, all those tiny baby chicks were everywhere, running behind their proud mothers. One year Ma kept missing babies; they were getting fewer and fewer each morning when she counted, and she found them scattered here and there, dead. She started watching, and Joe was the answer! He was dropping rocks on those chicks — squash! All that was left was feathers.

Everyone owned a dog for hunting rabbits and squirrels and watching the house. Our dog was Old Top. When Mother and Daddy were gone, Joe would tie tin cans full of gravel to Old Top's tail. Old Top would go full speed, barking with every breath as he ran to the mountain, scared to death. The faster he ran, the louder the noise got. I've no doubt he scattered the huckleberries — I felt we'd never see him again. But he always came home.

No wonder Joe grew into such a big boy; he nursed all the mothers in Poor Valley. Daddy would laugh about this. When Mother went to record or sing, Joe was left with Aunt Vangie, Dicey Thomas, or some other mother with a baby Joe's age. All babies were on the breast then.

He is now a big man — and as Gordon Bayes says, "Every inch a good man." I never saw anyone who didn't like Joe. He loves to tease you, to aggravate dogs and cats — they all run from Joe. He is a good singer and an excellent songwriter. You hardly ever see his equal on a guitar — he can play! He and his wife Nancy have three lovely daughters — Connie Joe, Lisa Ann, and Benita Jolene. A son, Jeffrey Lynn, lived one day and is buried next to my daddy. Joe and Nancy are divorced; he has since been remarried to Ruth Hartman and lives with her over in Tennessee.

I never saw Joe angry at anyone; he's easygoing like Mother. I beg him to record his songs, which he won't. He has always been good to me. He helped me on all three albums, "Joe and Janette Carter," "Storms Are on the Ocean," and "Howdoyedoo." He was the one who built a large music hall next to the store, "The Carter Family Fold," which now seats around eight hundred people.

I couldn't ask for a better brother. He's my friend. I ask his advice. He tunes my instruments. There'll never be but one Joe D. Carter.

The Singing Carters

My daddy learned music from Uncle Fland Bayes. He sang songs in church, so it came naturally for him and my mother to sing well. Maybelle Addington was Mother's first cousin; they grew up together. They were born and raised in and around Nickelsville — or Midway, Virginia. Mother and Daddy sang together before Maybelle married Uncle Ezra and joined them. I've heard Mother tell about their first personal appearance. They had been to Charlottesville, Virginia to visit Aunt Mae Hartsock, her sister. The car broke down, and they had no money to fix it. Daddy asked, "Sara, what can we do?" and she replied, "All I know to do is sing." So he booked a school for a music show that night and told a storekeeper to tell all who stopped by. They got money to have their car fixed and get home.

It was in August of 1927 that an ad appeared in the Bristol paper for artists to try out for a job to record songs — an unheard-of venture sponsored by a man named Ralph Peer from New York City. Daddy talked Maybelle and Mother into trying out for this job — there must be more money outside of Poor Valley, surely! So away they went in Uncle Eck's car—they had a flat on the way, Daddy said. There were several groups there, but the two chosen were the Carter Family and a young man by the name of Jimmy Rogers.

It was a very long, tiring day, waiting for them to come back from Bristol. Joe cried—he screamed for his mother and his milk. He wanted attention! Poor Gladys walked up and down State Street with him. Mrs. Peer tried to help. She fed him ice cream, and Joe's tears stopped, but he took the stomach ache from licking the ice cream. He couldn't understand this set-up at all. It was a day in which history was being made in the music world. Aunt Maybelle was expecting her first child in September, and today Helen will say, "I was there, too."

Uncle Lish Carter (Grandpa's brother) had his doubts about Bob and Molly's oldest son! "Doc" had done strange things, usually right backwards to other people. He never made plans but just rushed to different jobs head-on. He was an adventurous young man. For instance, Daddy built the house where Joe was born. Uncle Lish walked up the road to look it over when there was one room built and a fireplace outside the house. He never knew daddy was going to add on another room—only Daddy knew this. "Well, A. P. is going crazy," Uncle Lish said . "His fireplace is in the wrong place." So when Daddy calmly announced, "I am going to make records if Ralph Peer in Bristol likes our act," he said, "Send him out to Marion, Virginia [the mental hospital]. He's completely gone this time. His family will starve, no doubt!"

But they were accepted and Daddy started out on a new adventure—writing, collecting, and getting songs for a session about every three months. They took on the name, the "Carter Family." They had to practice, which was hard because A. P. and Sara had to drag three children along, and Uncle Ezra and Aunt Maybelle had three, too—Helen, June, and Anita. They had to work out music leads, time out a song to a certain second (not over three minutes), and try to keep Daddy still to sing bass when he was supposed to. Then there came the trips to the big cities. We stayed at Ma and Pa Carter's to wait until they returned. They had their songs ready, though, and sang so beautifully. In all their records, I never hear a mistake.

I remember listening to Daddy play the fiddle and the jew's-harp. He played well, though never on a record. Sometimes Uncle Grant went along and played fiddle, and Aunt Sylvia would fill in, too, if Maybelle or Mother couldn't go.

I guess of all his jobs, Daddy loved farming best, but singing was always on his mind. He sang a lot of hymns, as did Grandma Carter, going about her work singing "Amazing Grace" and "The Uncloudy Day." I suppose she sang to him when he was a baby, as I sing to mine; I guess all mothers do. Singing was frowned upon in Poor Valley, except in the church. It seemed everyone was supposed to sing hymns.

There were a few scattered square dances in the valley, but we couldn't go, as there might be drunks! Some stories of the Carter family have claimed my daddy drank, but he was the most sober man I ever knew. He hated whiskey; it was never in our home. We could dance at home, though — hoedown, buck dance, the Charleston, or hit the back step. I learned all this from the world's greatest dancer, my mother. I watched her feet; I watched her hands when she played the autoharp. At first I just listened, and I counted strokes to know when to change a chord. Then I wrote down songs and placed the chords above the words where I changed. I had a good memory, and besides this music was a constant thing at our house — just like castor oil, I got a lot of doses! If you are surrounded by music, you are bound to learn something! Always, after supper, there would be music. Maybelle worked out music leads on the guitar to a song they knew or wrote. If there was only one verse they knew, they wrote two more. All songs had three verses and a chorus; all timed out to three minutes. Words or music leads were all timed out to the very second to go onto a seventy-eight record.

They worked for about three months, writing, collecting, and learning the six or eight songs needed to record a session every six months. About twice a week they met to spend time really working at this music. Whenever Ralph Peer told them to go for their next recording session, they went, until they had finally got beyond Kingsport or Bristol, Virginia. All other work went on, too, but I'm quite sure that music was the better part of their lives.

As a rule, they practiced at Maybelle's house — how I loved to go there! With a furnace in their basement, Maybelle and Eck's was the warmest house in the valley. There was always a hired girl to do the work and to tend Helen, June, and Anita. Every meal looked like a Sunday dinner. Maybelle had a big piano in the corner of her living room, and she could play real well. She made a lot of candy, too. Uncle Eck was a mail clerk, gone a lot, so we children would sit and listen to Mother, Daddy, and Maybelle sing. My Aunt Maybelle was quite a lady, very lovely and always kind. Two of the kindest women in the world were she and my mother. She talked very little, like Mother. Daddy did the talking. They brought it all out in their music. First, when Mother, Maybelle, and Daddy walked out on stage, you gazed at their beauty. They dressed simply, and their songs were always so clear and distinct. Never, ever, a dirty joke — just music. They were good people! No wonder people loved them; they loved people in return. They poured their hearts into a school program, and they went to so many schools, dragging us children along. They made so little! We were always bought hamburgers or hotdogs. We six children, who sat and listened over and over again to these shows, never got tired of hearing them sing! I felt the same way thousands of others felt — that I was hearing three of the prettiest voices alive. God gave them talent, and they used it!

They wore their best clothes to perform. Daddy always had on a suit; he shed his work clothes gladly. He always walked out first onto the stage, Mother and Maybelle behind him. They would sit down in chairs or stand. There were even oil lamps back in the twenties and thirties in a lot of mountain schools. The program was about an hour and a half long, the charge (years ago) twenty-five cents for adults, five cents for children.

This early picture of Maybelle (with her guitar), Sara, and A. P. Carter was taken in front of Clinch Mountain in the 1920s.

MY CLINCH MOUNTAIN HOME

Far away on a hill
To a sunny mountainside,
Many years ago we parted
My little Ruth and I
From the sunny mountainside.

Chorus
Carry me back to old Virginia,
Back to my old mountain home.
Carry me back to old Virginia,
Back to my Clinch Mountain home.

In my hands I hold a picture
Of the old home far away.
The other one, my sweetheart,
I'm thinking of today
On the sunny mountainside.

Chorus

My father's old and feeble,
My mother's getting grey
I'm going back to Virginia,
And I expect to stay
At my old Clinch Mountain home.

Chorus

The Carter Family posed for pictures like this one, taken in Del Rio, Texas, in 1938, when they were beginning to tour and record songs like "My Clinch Mountain Home," written by my daddy. Below is a schoolhouse in Broadford, Virginia, where they performed; the man who sent me the photograph said that he had seen me dance on the table there!

All who were handicapped were allowed in free. They would say, "Now, Mr. Carter, I can pay." He would reply, "Let me sing for you, free; I want to do something for you." People listened so quietly to these hymns, love songs, and blues. The friends loved them! Daddy, Mother, and Maybelle would go home to where some kind people had asked them to stay for the night. Of the people they met then, their children still come by, saying, "Your parents stayed at my house." Our doors, too, were always open to the poor and the rich. "We seen Daddy come home with someone he picked up along the road," we'd say. "He's hungry; he needs a place to sleep." There was never any fear of strangers.

I remember that on one recording trip Mother and Maybelle went to get new dresses and hats. They bought blue dresses and coats to match with buttons all up the sleeves. They bought fur pieces too — fox furs to wear around their necks. These old fuzzy tails all sewed together and the eyes all glassy looked like the real thing! Joe (a little boy) took one look and decided he didn't want that animal around his mother's neck. He promptly jerked the tail off! Mama gently and firmly sewed it back, so the rip wouldn't show.

Maybelle was playing a Hawaiian guitar (she called it) on "Sweet Fern" and several other songs, but once when they were in New York at a recording session, she lost her "slide." Sara said, "Use my perfume bottle." It was smooth and would slide across strings, but Maybelle pressed too hard, and the bottle broke. "Lord, Sara, I've busted your perfume," she cried. "Blue Waltz" or "Evening in Paris" flooded the studio. Later Daddy recalled that Ralph Peer almost cracked up!

All three of them — Daddy, Mother, and Maybelle — had shiny black wavy hair and natural curls. They made a striking trio. Daddy was one of the tallest men in the Carter clan. Maybelle always looked like a fragile doll — she was so tiny — and Mother wasn't tall either, but she was very beautiful.

Once Ralph Peer and Anita come to Poor Valley. Eyes almost popped out on stems at that big black Cadillac driving up the dirt road. Hams were sliced, and old hens killed. Mother could wring a chicken's neck with not a care in the world. I'd hide my eyes and try to forget the ordeal. There were chickens and dumplings that day, and we used Maybelle's set of china.

We children were never pushed into music. Helen, June, and Anita worked each day at their music on a big piano. They were taught piano at school, where there was a music teacher, but I didn't have time to rehearse! I was always listening to the singing, though. There was happiness there. All their differences were forgotten if they were "lining out" a recording session. They were perfectionists and had to have it right! Music brought about this harmony; music certainly didn't cause their divorce! I feel they couldn't talk to each other; you have to be able to communicate to live together.

My daddy was dedicated to his music. He wanted me to sing; he told me once, "Write songs!" I only wrote two songs while my daddy was alive. He was the writer—I'm no songwriter! But in later years I've found myself expressing my thoughts in poetry, then finding a tune. If you listen closely, you can read or tell a person's life by his songs. I saw a reflection of unhappiness or being lonely in my daddy's songs, yet writing and singing were his happiness, as they are mine. It's no obsession; it's just there.

No wonder the Carter family was a success! Mother could sing like a lark. Daddy with his unusual bass voice could sing high or low—his range was unbelievable! And Aunt Maybelle, with those small, lovely hands all over a guitar, could bring out music no one else could ever master or believe. I'm their biggest fan! One of the happiest moments of my life was to book Sara and Maybelle Carter at my first A. P. Carter Memorial Day in 1975. I almost broke down in tears trying to describe or introduce these two ladies! It seemed even the birds listened to them sing that day, together again like they had sung so many times before. And they can still sing!

The Carter Family never realized what an impact they had on the music world. All they were trying to do was to provide for their families, but they brought happiness beyond measure to millions of people, both here and the world over. They loved, and I can understand why they are loved. Gladys, Joe, Helen, June, Anita, and I are trying; we are doing all we can do, but we are just milk. The cream of the crop has gone. Just like when my mother would churn cream to make butter—when the cream is gone, milk isn't much!

When the Carter Family broke up, Maybelle and her daughters formed a singing group and went out of the valley to work—Richmond, Knoxville, Missouri, and finally the Grand Old Opry in Nashville, Tennessee. They became world famous. Daddy was always proud of them. There was never any jealousy; there was only love. Even after Mother married Coy, they worked together. She and Daddy had a goal, and there were three children who belonged to both of them. He never spoke with anything but kindness of Maybelle and Mother. He told me after I moved back to the valley, "There needs to be one of my children to carry on my work—will you try?" How I could ever do that, I didn't know. I had two babies to raise, but I said, "Daddy, I will try."

If I worked until I fell over dead, if I could sing from now on, I could never repay my daddy, mother, or Maybelle for all they have done for me!

Adult Life and Music

One of my earliest memories is of hearing "Amazing Grace" and "The Uncloudy Day" being sung by Grandma Carter. I want these two songs to be sung at my funeral. I feel so close to God each time "Amazing Grace" is sung; if I'm troubled, I walk back to my Clinch Mountain and just sing this most beautiful of old songs! The first time I heard my Dale sing it I broke down in tears on stage at the Carter Fold. His voice was so beautiful, I felt chill bumps, and I knew my prayers, my dreams, and my work would go on through my child. Like Daddy's "little girl," he has learned to rely on God. You can't fail if He's there beside you!

I learned to play the autoharp from Aunt Sylvia and Mother. I never mastered the guitar, a stranger to me. All I can do on the autoharp is strum more or less. I've always wished I had talent like Joe — he can tune my harp or tune any instrument. I never saw a man with musical talent like my brother. Helen is outstanding, too. She seemed to always stand in the background, but she's like Joe — plays any instrument. All three of Maybelle's girls are very talented. Next to my mother and Maybelle, Anita has the most beautiful voice I have ever heard. She is a beautiful woman, too — as are June and Helen.

I started my musical career as a buck dancer, or doing the Charleston, hitting the back step. I was six years old, and I still remember the little Indian suit my daddy bought me. It had a headband of feathers, shiny buttons, and bells on my trouser legs that jingled while I danced "Red Wing." Mother sang, and Maybelle played the guitar. I stood on a school stage atop a table to dance, and I got my first payday. I was thrown dimes, pennies, nickels — the most money I had ever seen! Some kind man threw me fifty cents, and I said, "Daddy, what a big one!" I remember a silver toy horse from a Cracker Jack box — this was cherished more than my earnings.

Helen and I started singing together when she was eight and I was twelve. I played the autoharp, she the guitar. I remember once my picks flew off my fingers; you can't play without picks! I laid my harp down, went and got them, never did quit singing, came back on stage, and sat down, still singing. Everyone laughed at me. Helen and I had a lot of good times.

I was always quiet and shy, but I had Mother, Daddy, Maybelle, and Helen on stage behind me. So if I made a mistake, they could help. The first time I ever walked out on stage alone, just me and the harp, was at Eastern Tennessee State University in Johnson City. I felt sure I was going to faint. I prayed, "God go with me, I can't walk out alone." He went with me, and I got through that night.

Thirteen was a number that kept appearing in my life. When I was thirteen years of age, Helen and I were singing together and I was saving the money I got — dimes, quarters, half dollars. Gladys had married Milan and moved to Mendota, taking Joe with her. There was just Daddy and I — I was running the house, or trying to, anyway. I wanted my own harp; I had always used my mother's. I saved all of thirteen dollars and gave it to Daddy for this music box! He went off, and I kept looking down the road for his return. As I said, my daddy was a strange man, a person whose mind

The picture of me with my autoharp was taken in the late 1960s, after I had taken up music again. Above, my daddy at the same time, in front of the home place, now Gladys's house in Poor Valley. The picture of Joe and his first wife, Nancy, was taken around 1950.

wandered at times. He used my money to buy little baby chickens—the kind that would grow up, lay eggs, make dumplings, and be sold for groceries. That was one of the most hurtful days of my life. I had to save all over again, but the next time I got my harp. I guess Daddy couldn't stand another day of tears!

In Texas I was put in school along with Joe. The school was so large, I kept getting lost. The students there laughed at my southern drawl and would say, "Will you talk?" Then they'd laugh at my accent. For one who always loved school, this was a hurtful ordeal in a strange place. I never felt so alone! I missed my beautiful hills of home. I was in love, too, with Jimmy Jett, which was one of the reasons I had been jerked up in the first place by Daddy. But I worried him and myself sick with crying, so I was sent home to stay with Grandma. I quit school and married. Now I look back and realize that I didn't have one lick of sense. Everyone was in tears—Grandma, Sib, Gladys. Maybelle said, "Janette, you are too young. You are a child." She was sixteen when she was married, as was my mother, but I was too young! Well, I found out I was. Just because you can keep house, work, and make your own money doesn't make you "grown up." My husband and I moved to Bristol, Virginia. It almost broke my daddy's heart; all he said was "You have had so little happiness, I hope you will be happy." I endured eighteen years of city life, and I found out why people divorce. If you can't get along, it is the best way. By then I understood a lot and only loved my mother and daddy more. To admit failure hurts so very deeply—my divorce left a scar that never will heal.

I was lost, so I came home to Daddy. He built me a small house and moved in with me, Rita, and Dale. My Don was sixteen and stayed with his father to continue school. I hold no bitterness or hatred toward their father—my beautiful children were worth it all—and we parted friends.

There were just three years with Daddy. He loved his grandchildren, and when I moved back home, they seemed to brighten his life! The most peaceful years of my life were spent with Daddy, Rita, and Dale on "Happy Hill," the name we gave our house and the acre of land where it stands.

I worked in restaurants, in factories, in fields, in schools. I cooked and washed dishes to be near my children; I cleaned houses. I had to work to raise my family. Daddy helped, but soon he was gone. So I prayed for strength, for health, and for work to give them what they needed. I wanted them to have much more than I ever had, but it was very hard to even keep food on the table! I hung on. I prayed and cried hundreds of times. I kept charging along like old Custer. I worked harder at being a good mother than I had at any other job I'd ever done. My beautiful children were mine; no one but God could take them. I was their world; just like my daddy was to me, I am to them!

My music was put aside at age sixteen, until I was married the second time in 1965. There were small amounts of "music work." Daddy, Mother, Joe, and I recorded some in the fifties for Acme Records, but my heart and my life were devoted to my children— my beautiful three, "my little tribe," I called them. I didn't want to leave them; I'd spent my childhood seeing far too little of my mother and daddy.

Mother came home once a year from California. I saw her very little. How I missed her! But three thousand miles is a long way off—if I got to Kingsport or Bristol, I was doing wonders!

One year, Gladys and Milan bought a brand new car. They were going to California to see Mother and Coy. So I decided to take Rita and Dale, who were all of five and three years old. We were five days on the road. They screamed, they fought, they vomited. Rita kept crying for Happy Hill—she felt each city was the end of the world. Dale kept holding his breath and fainting. They cried for five solid days, and all three of us staggered into California from sheer exhaustion! I promptly turned my children over to their "Mama Jake" and took to my bed. It was Christmas, but there wasn't snow like there is in Virginia. Poor little Dale started worrying: "Santa may not know where I am. I'm not where I usually am at Christmas." He cried and screamed, as Coy

combed the hills to come up with a tree which had to be lighted so
Santa could find the house. Every time Mother turned the lights
off Dale cried, "Santa has to see the lights!" So I lay in bed and
watched lights flicker off and on all night, to quiet a small boy.
Like the lightning bugs that flickered when I was a small girl, the
gentle glow soothed away the tears. I spent another Christmas
with Mother and promised God, "If I ever go again with these
two, they will be grown and take me." They've not taken me yet!
I'll just keep my feet on Poor Valley soil. The two times I traveled
by plane, I was numb with fright—but my mother was near death,
and I felt I was closer to God up there. I prayed all the way to
California, "Don't let this plane crash." Well, I made it. It didn't
crash.

My children, Donald William, Rita Janette, and James
Delaney Jett, are by my first husband, James L. Jett. Their daddy
and I are friends. Like all mothers, I could write a book about each
child, especially Dale, who was the exploring type and so like my
daddy in his ways that at times I feel tears in my eyes. Need I say
they are my reason for living? But I'll not go into my children's
lives. That would make three books, and though they are my life,
this book is about my life when I was a child and how it feels to be
part of a famous family who never felt famous at all.

My Donald William Jett was born in 1941. Strange as it may
seem, they said I sang while he was being born! We lived in
Bristol, Virginia, and Don was born at home. I was attended by a
very worried Dr. Bowers. I no doubt did sing "Amazing Grace"—
I was, to my way of thinking, in the most terrible pain I had ever
endured! For fourteen hours I cried and prayed for my baby to be
born. My mother was crying and saying, "If possible, I'd have the
baby." They finally put me to sleep with chloroform. My mother
and Mrs. Jett ran out of the house, as my mother thought that
when people start singing while they're giving birth, they are near
death! That dose of chloroform, I felt, saved my life. My husband
said, "I'll never go through this again and watch. She'll be in a
hospital." The next two, Rita and Dale, were born at Bristol

BOUQUET OF DANDELIONS

Thirty-one winters have come and gone
Since first I gazed on my oldest son.
A ray of bright sunlight, so close to me
The years they passed swiftly,
    soon there were three.

The long golden summers, soon you were grown.
My fondest memories, they linger on.
A little boy smiling, so eager to please,
A bouquet of dandelions handed to me.

Above is Donald, my eldest,
for whom I wrote this song;
below are Rita and Dale,
and myself as a young mother
holding Dale and Rita.

When I grow up now, and all on my own,
I'll buy pretty dresses and things for your home.
You are the sweetest mother I know
Instead of dandelions, you'll have a rose.

Though you have left me, you never have changed.
So kind, so gentle, always the same.
Not only mother, but others you please.
Why, he is a good man! You plainly can see.

A golden-haired angel runs through the door.
A ray of bright sunlight, I'm lonely no more.
"Gran-Gran, I love you"—through tears I do see
A bouquet of dandelions, handed to me.

Memorial Hospital. Dr. Bowers told me later that their daddy had begged for a dose of chloroform, too. It was quite an ordeal!

My Don has always been so close to his mother. Well, all three come to me, thank God. They can come to me — I'm there to listen, to try to solve all problems, to give love. Don loved pets. He was our only child for thirteen years, and we tried to give him what he wanted, so I bought him a duck at Easter. It grew up, and wherever Don walked outside, Waddles did, too. One day I looked out to see Don carrying his duck, her head flapping loose across his little arm. "She's been killed, Mother, by a car," he said. "Her neck is broken." He was crying, and I was, too. "You must do something," he said. To ease his hurt, we had a funeral — the full works. Waddles was buried in a clean box under a pine at the end of the garden. We even picked flowers. "Mother, you must sing," Don said. So there I was singing "Amazing Grace" over Waddles — but it made Don feel better. The neighbors thought I was crazy, but my son's thoughts were more dear to me than those of anyone else, and if singing brought him less hurt, I sang. The feel of my babies in my arms at the close of a day, while I sang softly and gently rocked each one to sleep, was the most peaceful feeling of being loved and knowing they were mine.

My Donald is married to Phyliss Dillard. They have one child, Malissia Ann. How I love this little angel — she calls me Gran-Gran. I don't recall my Don ever being anything but a good boy, always very quiet and obedient. He favors his daddy, while Rita and Dale are fair like the Carters. My tall, dark, handsome Don, my first born, naturally seems closer, being the oldest. It's been a long time since my Don brought me a "bouquet of dandelions." I wish the whole world was made up of men like my Donald William Jett — what a good world it would be!

Born in 1954, my beautiful Rita Janette with her golden curls and her brown eyes was, I thought (then, as now), the prettiest baby I ever laid eyes on. I almost died when she was born. I love her, as any mother loves her only daughter. She is something!

Rita is married to Robert Forrester, and they have a son,

Rita and Dale in Poor Valley.

RITA AND DALE

There's a cabin at the foot of Clinch Mountain,
Not far from the place I was born.
Gentle breezes blow through the cedars,
Singing birds wake you up in the morn.
As a young girl, I left the old homestead
For years in the city to dwell.
My latter days spent in Poor Valley
With my lovely Rita and Dale.

Chorus
I rocked them to sleep in the twilight,
Tucked them in safely and well.
Not a diamond that ever shined,
More precious than Rita and Dale.

Hand in hand through childhood they
    wandered,
My dear little boy and a girl,
Surrounded by friends and relations,
The kindest ones in the whole world.
Clear waters that flow through the
    meadows,
Wild flowers, they bloom in the dale.
A haven of rest in the evening,
They called it my happy hill.

Chorus

Golden curls lay pressed in a Bible,
Their little shoes covered with bronze.
The long years of struggling and praying—
I sometimes feel so alone.
The morning dawns—now I hear footsteps—
A young man, a lady, I see.
Dear voices—"Mother, I love you,"
Is all the thanks I'll ever need.

Chorus

*My children grew up quickly!
Left, at her wedding, Rita
with her brothers Don and
Dale. Above, on the same day,
Rita and her husband Bob
Forrester, with Uncle Ermine
between. Right is Don and his
wife Phyliss. Below right is
Don's daughter Malissia
Ann, and below left is
Rita's son Joseph Justin.*

Joseph Justin, a beautiful little boy who thinks his "Maw-Maw" is quite a lady. If all people loved me like Justin does, I would be well loved! I suppose Rita clings to her mother most of all. We share secrets; I tell her my problems. She's always trying to help Mother. "A son is a son till he takes a wife, but a daughter is a daughter all her life." Thank God for my beautiful Rita!

James Delaney, born in 1957, is my youngest. I call him Jimmy Dale. He is named after his two grandfathers. My daddy will never die, as long as Dale lives. How I ever raised Dale, I don't know; he was into everything! This handsome lad could charm a black snake. He loves everyone, and everyone loves him. I know we spoiled him, as we did Don and Rita. He's been lectured quite a bit, my Dale. He used to say, "Please, Mother, get a switch — no lecture." I punished my children very little; I'd sit them down and explain right and wrong. I never believed in all those wild cherry switches. They hurt! My children are, to me, like three precious gems that all the gold in China couldn't buy.

From the time I moved back to the valley from Bristol, Virginia twenty-six years ago, when Rita was only three and my Dale a baby of eleven months, there has been so much grief, so much hard work, and so many hard times that to even write about it all hurts, so I'll try not to mention this period of my life. I barely survived on what was given to me for their support by their daddy. My time went to my babies — they needed me. I felt that if they couldn't have both parents, they needed their mother even more. The years seemed very long and lonely. I went to church and to Kingsport about twice a month. Otherwise I stayed at home most of the time.

It seems that all my life I was searching for happiness, for something with permanent roots, for security. Most of all I needed love. My children loved and needed me, so I gave my time and my love to them as freely as I breathed.

My best time, during this period, was when I went to work at nearby Hilton School as a cook. Rita and Dale were there, so I could be close to them if they needed Mother. I worked part-time

THE OLD DIRT ROAD

There's memories of a little boy,
A fishing pole, a dog who's brave,
Who walks barefooted through the meadows.
Poor Valley dirt — shadows lying in the shade.

It takes a lot of "growing-up."
I will help you — I will pray!
A hundred paths will twist and wind.
Just keep walking — there's one; it's paved!

You'll shed a lot of helpless tears —
Mother, she will see or hear.
All too soon, one day you stand alone —
Where do I go from here?

A thousand dreams go through your mind —
Callous hands, there's few that go untouched.
It takes a lot of looking
To find a diamond in the rough!

Life is a tall and shaky ladder.
To reach the top, look to the sky,
Someone keeps your balance steady.
Remember others; they too have tried!

One who walks the way he wants to
And cares not who understands,
He's searching for his destiny —
With God's help he'll make a man!

*Don as a teenager standing
by the dirt road just before
it was paved in 1957;
Dicey Thomas's house is in
the background.*

after school in a nearby restaurant as a cook. I always worked more than one job. I also went to schools and put on music programs and charged a small amount. I took a percent and gave the school a percent. I've always loved schoolchildren, and I felt closer to my daddy when I put on these school programs, as I remembered going to schools as a child to hear him sing.

In September of 1965 I married Dempsey J. Kelly, nick-named Jack. His parents had rented a lot from me to set a trailer on. Little did I know that I was making yet another mistake in my life. Jack and I are now divorced. I've always felt as though I'm the one who causes "so much worry." I don't mean to do this, but my life has always been rough—I guess it's been my fault. As I said, God and my children keep me going along. I make myself content with simple pleasures, like a walk in the wood or waking up each day and saying, "Thank you, God, for another day." Dale always said, "Someone watches over my mother." I'll go on the road, even though I can't even tune my autoharp. Someone will help me, I know. I can always sing without one, if it gets that bad, and I can still dance, which I seldom do anymore.

I try to write songs; I never make myself write, but tunes come into my head at odd times, while I'm walking or working. Most of them are based on true happenings or how I feel. As a rule, writing is easy for me. My first song, "Pretty Raindrops," I wrote in about ten minutes' time. Tunes come and go in phrases till I just go into my room and stay there until I finish the song. My room is a place I go to to be alone—like a stump over in Clinch Mountain that I almost wore out when Rita and Dale were small, sitting on it, praying all alone.

Music brings back the "good memories" of my life. It seems to me, looking back, that I was never truly a child. The Bible says, "The good men do lives after them." Naturally, you cling to the good memories, though my life has been a lonely life.

A KIND GENTLE MAN

Long, long ago
In the Bible we're told
A baby was born
In a far distant land.
Mary prayed on her knees,
Dear God, help me please!
May He grow up to be
A kind gentle man!

Chorus
And oh, how I love Him,
My Savior, my friend.
And though I'm unworthy,
His blessing descend—
The sunshine each morn,
Many wonders I see,
Even air that I breathe
From this kind, gentle man.

And though He walks lonely,
Forsaken by friends,
He speaks not in anger,
A hand He will lend!
The foxes have holes,
The birds they have trees,
But my dearest Jesus
Had nowhere to sleep!

Chorus

And when but a young man,
All alone and afraid,
He gave His life freely,
So a world could be saved.
On a cross He was hung,
Not a wrong He had done.
Only loved every one—
This kind gentle man!

Chorus

My daughter Rita was baptized in the Holston River in 1965.

The old store as it looked in 1954 — in front are my mother, my daddy, and me.

Music at the Store

It took me a long time to realize I have a talent, that God had given me one! It never occurred to me, while Mother, Daddy, and Maybelle lived, to devote my life to music. They were there while I was busy working at any work to survive and support my children. Paul in the Bible said, "Look to the future — look ahead and not back." What is past is gone like water under a bridge; it flows on somewhere else. So when my marriages failed, I turned to music. It's a shelter to me — my happiest memories are music. I love all music, but I like the kind my family sang best. They poured their hearts into their work. My music is like the love I give my children, my friends, my family, and my God. I give all of me!

The turning point came one year as late summer was turning into fall. I was sitting on the steps, looking out over the valley, feeling pressures of hills — my future looked dim. Inside of me lay a promise I had made to my daddy, "I will carry on your work." The old store was there going to waste, and I couldn't even finish my house — it needed repair. I needed so much! My pay at the school was so little. The idea came to me: music. Why not have music? In the store! Maybe I could keep my promise and add some income! I told my husband and children, "In one month, there will be music in the store." They looked at me as though I were going insane! But Jack and I threw out dirt, tobacco stalks, old furniture — that store was a storage room for junk! I called the three newspapers in the area and said, "I want a story done on this." They thought I was a little crazy, but they sent reporters.

We built benches and bleachers. I plunged into debt alone. I'd asked my mother to loan me money, but she refused. I realize now that she felt that I was making a grave mistake. I guess I've always been the rebellious one — I didn't listen!

So August 24, 1974 rolled around, and the store was cleaned and shining. The papers had printed stories about my show coming up. I sat on the front step of the old store and prayed, "If it be thy will, God, let me succeed. I promise you I'll keep rules to keep the shows orderly — no drinking or profanity. They will be a memorial to my family, the Carters, and to their kind of music." I have kept my promise to God and to my daddy. I have tried and succeeded.

The cars started coming up the valley to the "little store." Soon the crowd in the store spilled out the door, and we moved out into the front yard. Admission was one dollar; children were admitted free. The first night, one hundred ninety-six dollars were taken in to pay the booked artists, my friends Jean and Lee Schilling, and a blind singer named Sylvia Sammons.

I worked endlessly, it seemed. I made my first posters myself and used plain rough paper. I took them and posted them near homes, in stores, in filling stations — my music had very little advertising but its reputation has grown mostly through word of mouth

I have met a lot of people in my time, and a lot of musicians have become my friends. I started asking them to come and perform. I paid them a percentage, and the store admission was so small that no money was made. If bands came to play from outside

*This is a love song I've sung at several weddings; it's also how I'd
have liked my own life to be! My brother Joe and I still sing
together.*

LIVING WITH MEMORIES

A boy, a girl, with auburn curls,
Childhood sweethearts were we,
So very near; in laughter or tears
I've loved you so tenderly.
Wherever you go, my dear,
   I will go,
Walking so close to thee
Down life's long and rugged road,
Living with memories.

Chorus
A winning smile, the clear blue
   eyes,
Dark and wavy hair.
The tender touch, I love so much,
And you're always there —

To hold my hand and understand,
So much, a part of me.
Together we've weathered a whole
   lot of storms,
Living with memories.

The youthful years have passed
   away
Like falling leaves from a tree.
The children's steps no longer echo.
Again there's just you and me.
If you go first and I remain,
No matter how lonely I'll be,
I'll spend the rest of my life alone,
Living with memories.

Chorus

the valley, I kept them in my home and I fed them. I still worked at the school, but I spent my weekends at the store. I brought in a lot of talent that had never even been on stage! There's a lot of talent in Scott County.

The first publicity I received besides the stories in the local papers, the *Johnson City Chronicle,* the *Bristol Herald Courier,* and the *Kingsport Times,* was an article done by *Smithsonian.* I feel their help brought a lot of people from outside of Virginia to this tiny place, the home of the famous Carter Family.

At first, there was no sound system, but the crowds got larger, and I needed two microphones anyway. I made no money in the first two years of business; I just built up the business. I laid a foundation built on faith. If I had to refuse to let a drunk in my building or someone who kept making too much noise, if I needed to stop all this nonsense, I did! I always made my rules very clear. I put up a plaque with my feelings about music. Some man from New York said, "If I read this when I'd been drinking, at once I would have become sober!" He said he "almost bowed" to a lady who had so much faith and was brave enough to put the rule on the wall for all to see!

I am a person who sometimes makes decisions very fast and on short notice. I was very tired from my work and my music — my marriage was unhappy — so one day I simply called the school and said, "I'll not be back to work. I'm giving you a month's notice to find another person to cook. I'm going to devote all my time to music." I tried not to feel apprehensive about such a big step. If a doubt arose, I just prayed, "Help me, God." I'd been having shows every other Saturday night, so I started having programs every Saturday night. I didn't listen to all the rumors that said, "You'll never make it; that's too much music." The crowds got larger, never smaller. A lean-to was added on to seat more people and to add a small concession.

I came in for my share of personal criticism, too. I live in a small community, and I was frowned upon by some who felt, "Women don't run a small music hall." I worked very hard; I cried a lot of tears. I was having a lot of worries, but something inside me kept saying, "I will try." I remembered my promise.

I decided to have a festival, a one-day event — a "Memorial Day" to my daddy. So even though I didn't know how to start, I started. I had no stage outside, no platform for a clogging team, nothing but a field. I knew the store could never hold the people, even with just one band. I was going to use three or four bands and some dancers. I set a date and worked to get everything done by August 1975.

I had seen flatbed army trucks at places in Kingsport where there were musical events. So why not call the National Guard? I called. They said, "There's no way we can let you use a truck. You have no sponsor. You're a woman out of the clear blue sky who wants a truck to try to put on a festival in Poor Valley!" I forget the man's name, but I called him till he gave up in despair! He finally said, "If you have the courage to try, I'll give you permission." So two days before my event, two of the largest flatbed army trucks you ever saw came up Poor Valley Road with a crew of men to set it all up! It looked about as sad, I suppose, as my daddy dragging the sawmill up Poor Valley's road. I've no doubt been the subject in a lot of homes that have "after-supper talks" about Janette Carter!

I still had no stage for my dancers, the Southern Appalachian Cloggers. My cousin kindly said that I could use the trees on his land. I sent my husband to saw them down, and he got on forbidden land, so I paid out sixty dollars for a few pine logs that we trimmed and dragged to the field. We covered them with rough plywood for the dancers. That cost me around three hundred dollars, plus blistered hands and a strained back. I wound up in the hospital, but my show was presented — my first job of directing a festival which has become a yearly event in Poor Valley. I came out broke, but I paid all I booked and I learned something. I learn every year, the hard way — by experience!

My brother Joe is a carpenter. He said, "I'll build a building for the music. We'll be partners." After two years, I began to get

I wrote this song in Pine Woods Camp, near Boston, when I was homesick; it's my way of thanking God for each new day. Here the store, behind my mother and me, has a fresh coat of paint shining in the morning sun. Below, the inside of the store comes alive with music played by Bill Hicks and the Red Clay Ramblers, and my old Aunt Ora, right, loves to sit and listen as much as my little cousin Mark Carter!

MORNING SUNLIGHT

Awake, the whole new world is dawning.
The sun is shining through the pines.
Awake, the rooster is now crowing,
The air is purer, you will find.
Awake, the old hound dog is whining,
Looking for his morning meal.
Jesus kept you through the darkness.
Start your day — He loves you still!

In the valley, neighbor's rising.
I can see a dove forlorn
Sitting on my front steps praying
For the rain to bathe the corn.
There's a feeling — oh, so restful —
Dew drops falling from the trees.
I can hear the sounds of morning —
Another day, I welcome thee!

Though I'm old, I still see beauty
In every leaf and tree,
See the minnows in the creek beds,
Flowing gently to the sea.
I will greet each day so thankful
God has been a friend to me!
I will do just what He says to —
Morning sunlight, shine on me.

The Carter Family Fold Music Hall, built in 1976, where "old-time music" is presented every Saturday night. The building is really a memorial to the Carter Family—A. P., Sara, and Maybelle. (Photos by Adam Klein)

"notice." The large hall was built by family, neighbors, and musicians—all free labor except for the work that required hired help, such as pouring the concrete dance floor. The electric work was done by Coy, my stepfather. Cross ties make the seats lie like steps up a steep hill, and it's all enclosed by a big roof and rough lumber sides. It resembles a very large barn.

My music goes on. It's been over eight years since I opened my first show in the little store. It sits quietly by the large "Carter Family Fold" music hall, yet it is very much a part of the whole operation. When I directed the first show in the Fold and looked out at that large space, I thought, "How on earth can I make these people feel close to me?" In the store I could reach out and almost touch their hands; here, I felt so alone. But I learned that you just open your arms wider, and there's enough love in your heart to love all people. When I walk on stage, I still feel as I did when I was thirteen years old.

I have friends who have stood by me through all trials. Financially speaking, my greatest help is Johnny Cash. But there's other help besides money. I've always had so little, yet I feel I'm the richest woman in Poor Valley. Looking back, I realize I'm fortunate. I never started my music until I was past fifty years old—it took me that long to find my destiny! I don't blame my parents, my broken marriages, my ex-husbands—I blame no one but Janette for my failures and my unhappiness. I paid my debts in life; I made my own bed. It's not a bed of roses, this music or my life—roses have thorns, too, you know! My hope is to go on and to do a job that will make my children proud enough that they will carry on when I'm gone. My happiness is being at peace at last. I have my grandchildren, my children, my friends and family, and first of all, my Jesus!

The grandchildren of Molly and Bob Carter gather now, at the Homecoming in August. Lois, Jack, Juanita, Mary Ann (Robert is gone), Ruth, Blanche, Esther, R. M., Patsy, Benny, Scotty, Fern, W. L., Roger, Jim and Bob (Sylvia's twins), and of course, Helen, June, and Anita. They are scattered all over

Virginia and Tennessee, as well as other states; we see each other less and less.

Gladys Ettaleen — called G. G. by Nancy Flo — still lives nearby with her daughter, her daughter's husband Johnny, and their children, Dewanna, Yolanda, Mark, and Dana. My G. G. still gives advice, still makes my dresses. She's still there when I'm sick in the hospital (and I'm in and out quite often), or whenever I need her. She's just like the Rock of Gibralter, this good woman — the strength of this family! Milan, her husband, I love like I do Joe. To me, he's a brother, one of the best men I ever met. Gladys is the lucky one!

Joe is now my singing buddy. He's a chip off the old block. He writes beautiful songs, and he's mastered the guitar in a class all his own. There are some chips in this family — some polish left yet.

Helen, my friend, seems like a fragile lily, but she's a very strong person. She lost a son, Kenny, but Kevin, Danny, and David will help her. They will carry on in music.

Valerie June could be a movie star! Grandpa said, "She's got enough brass to make a tea kettle." She's the famous one, with more than her share of talent and beauty. What's more, she married a superstar — leave it to June! And Johnny Cash is no fool. A. P. Carter and Ezra found two wildwood flowers in Scott County, so Johnny took notice and found his June here. She's his shining star, his angel! He may have been right when he said, "These Carters are the salt of the earth." Johnny is my friend — I thank God for him. It doesn't matter to me if he's poor or a millionaire — I love this giant of a man! June has Carlene and Rosie to carry on the Carter name and a son, John Carter Cash.

Anita, the beauty of the Carter family, has a voice that makes you think of angels singing. She's come a long way since she slept in guitar cases when she was small. She started early — only six. I love her Lorrie and Jay like they belong to me. Last, but not least, there's no one like Uncle Ermine and Aunt Ora. They live at the old home place. Ermine and Sib are all that are left of Daddy's

A FRIEND

The one who's always thought of
In every joy or sorrow.
The one for whom I pray ,
Each day, each night, tomorrow.
There's a few who know my every
      thoughts,
Although I'm seldom near them.
I know if life gets very rough,
They will know I need them.
My world is full of thorns and flowers —
Just love them, they will grow.
True friends like jewels are as rare
As crocuses blooming in the snow.
My Jesus is my shining star;
My very life depends on Him.
There have to be some dimmer stars
That shine close by until the end.
My dreams, my hopes belong to me.
I own no gold to give or lend —
Thank God! All I have to do is give
      my self,
And I am loved by friends.

*Two musician friends — Red Rector and Bill Clifton — and I
stand in Poor Valley in front of Addington Gap.*

people — Aunt Sylvia lives in Kentucky. I depend on Uncle Ermine; he fills in for Daddy. I look to see the truck coming down the road on Saturday night to the music show. My Aunt Ora is crippled with arthritis, but she does more work than any woman who is in good health. She doesn't give up! She still milks and churns. I go over and just stick my feet under her table and say, "I want some milk and bread." It tastes like Grandma's milk and bread. This couple is content with the land, the peace of the valley, not a lot of money, just the feeling of knowing God. They help neighbors — Uncle Ermine has tended more sick and dug more graves than any man in Scott County. He's also a great hunter; my Dale went with him and had to run to keep up. He knows every foot of Clinch Mountain and every riverbank. He's a friend to people, the kind of man that does a job from the goodness of his heart. God dwells in him.

For myself, I'm happy here at the foot of Clinch Mountain. To a passing stranger, my life is very simple. What little wealth I have was left to me by my daddy and saved from what I've earned singing in colleges and schools and working in restaurants. I've never had anything expensive but always tried to make myself content with what I had, and I've succeeded. My happiness is knowing my children are grown; God answered my constant prayer to let me live to see them grown and on their own.

There's no place to me like Scott County, the hills of Virginia, the ever-changing scenes of Clinch Mountain. I am growing old, but worrying about that only makes you get older quicker, so I don't worry. I have my children who love me, and above all else, I have a friend, Jesus, who walks with me wherever I go. I love my neighbors, though they're the world's worst when it comes to talking and gossiping, as all small communities are. Everyone knows your business, but no matter — ask them to help you, they are there!

I neglect my God most. I don't go to church like I should, but we have "talks" each day. Wherever I walk, He walks. He's my faith, my shelter, my strength. He's there. That to me is the greatest gift of all—to turn around, no matter where you are, and to feel there's someone close! He's closer to me each year since my mother and daddy are gone. I always fear losing Gladys, Joe, or my children. If I were to dwell on all this, I believe I would surely die, but God is there! So I'm devoting my life here on earth to keeping, or trying to keep, my family's songs alive. Everything I do is in some way an attempt to repay them for all they have done for me. I am proud of them! Music brings people together. "A family that prays together stays together"—the same applies to singing. There's happiness in songs and music.

The Carter Fold is my way of trying to keep my mother and daddy's memories close to me. It's been hard, but I didn't expect it to be easy! I feel happy in my music. If I felt I was doing wrong, there would be no music. I can truthfully say that it has brought those I love closer to me. No wonder I work so hard at my music—it surrounds me with love! My living and God—I have so much to be thankful for. I really do!

I love to look down on the old store where my music started and feast my eyes on the mountains.